BIBLICAL SCHOOLS

FOR

COVENANT CHILDREN

Gregory J. Maffet

SIGNAL

Copyright 1987
by
Gregory J. Maffet

BIBLICAL SCHOOLS FOR COVENANT CHILDREN

ISBN 0-941221-00-8

SIGNAL   Reformed Educational Publishing and Consultant Co.
7320 W. 130th St., Middleburg Heights, OH   44130

Dedicated to
Margaret
our parents
and our
special friends

Table of Contents

PART III
A Biblical School - Theory and Practice

PART IV
Biblical Schools for Covenant Children
The Call *133*

Foreword

Here is a book to buy and read!

Dr. Maffet, no stranger to Christian education or to the study of the Scriptures, here put together a book that probes the foundations of biblical teaching and learning and points the way to more consistent thought and practice.

This book is a must for every Christian school teacher, parent and administrator in America.

It is my hope that Dr. Maffet will continue to write in this field, building on the foundations he has laid in this book.

Jay E. Adams
Valley Center
1987

Author's Note

In 1972 I was a first-year teacher in a prominent southern Christian school. My administrator thought that I ought to have a good handle on Christian education since I was a recent graduate of a Christian college and had graduated from an excellent Christian high school. God had blessed me with Christian parents and a fundamental church. My testimony and enthusiasm for Christian education was strong.

By most standards that first year of teaching was a success. I had covered all the curriculum content in the history, economics and Bible courses. My students had done well and I had established excellent rapport with most of the students, parents and other school personnel. It seemed that I was on top of my little world.

Then the Spirit of God began to ask me questions. *What makes your teaching different from non-Christian teaching? What is your philosophy of education? What is the relationship between doctrine and teaching, between the Bible and learning? Can you justify, explain, or defend your view of Christian education in opposition to other views of education?*

Sadly, I realized that my Christian teaching was nothing more than a flood of facts being taught in a moral environment. Biblical principles were applied whenever I could think of an application, but this was a rare occurrence for what did God have to do with the fact that the Declaration of Independence was written by Thomas Jefferson?

The Holy Spirit began to teach me. I enrolled in graduate school, read hundreds of books, and studied my Bible. New ideas took hold. Concepts such as integration, Christian world and life views, Christian perspective, Truth, Apologetic, and integral-learning took shape in my mind. My teaching began to change. The biblical perspective stood out in complete, all encompassing, contrast to other perspectives. The covenant relationship which God established with me through Christ turned the dark world into light. Not only was God to control my moral life, He was to be Lord of my mind and all my activity, to rule every thought and hold every action captive to the obedience of Christ.

ix

For fifteen years I have wrestled with the various aspects of Christian education. For twenty years I have been a Christian student, teacher or administrator in a Christian school. Throughout these years I have explored and observed education, particularly Christian school education. It is my hope that the Christian philosophy of education contained in this book will be the light of Christ to those who read it.

The twentieth century has been marked by the phenomenal growth of Christian schools. Although some Christian schools existed when this century began, their initial growth was slow. It was not until the period between 1960 and 1985 that Christian school education escalated rapidly with the opening of thousands of new schools.

The impact of these new Christian schools is evident in all areas of life. Churches and parent organizations have built school complexes; teaching staffs have been formed; school equipment purchased; specifically Christian curriculum and texts have been designed and published. Thus, there has been an economic shift in production and marketing which affects even such areas as the design and architecture of churches, and the demand upon colleges for Christian teachers who are able to biblically instruct our youth.

Growth has been so rapid that Christian school leaders have been preeminently busy with the practical affairs of organizing and running schools. Scholarly work has been delayed by the urgent need to raise finances, secure buildings, hire teachers and develop routine school procedures. The successful Christian school is characterized as being well organized and smoothly run in a moral environment which is strict and traditionally Christian. In brief, a good Christian school appears orderly and abides by fundamental rules and regulations which are believed to be biblically moral. With this goal in mind, most Christian school leaders have adopted curriculum, teaching methods and a learning theory which appear to be compatible with orderliness and traditional morality. In other words, the means of Christian education are considered to be Christian if they result in orderly and moral Christian schools. Hence, a form of Christianized pragmatism (if it works, use it) has rooted itself within the Christian school movement.

Because of the rapid growth, the tyranny of the urgent, and existing educational traditions, many Christian school leaders have simply Christianized the secular school system. Christian schools have been constructed in the image of secularized public school systems. Student activities, administrative procedures, student evaluation, classroom design and the teaching-learning process have been modeled after America's public schools. To be sure, Christian morals and the marks of Christian love are integrated into the curriculum and life. Yet, within the Christian school movement, there remains the fruit of secular humanism; the roots and branches of humanistic thinking have not been totally removed.

Part I of this book discusses the very foundation of the Christian school movement. The basic question Christian school leaders must answer is "Why?" Why do Christians believe that Christian schools are necessary for their children? I believe the answer lies in the covenant God has made with His people of faith. The ultimate and conclusive reason which fully justifies the necessary existence of Christian schools rests completely upon God and the covenant relationship which He has made with His people which results in their grateful response. Christians, in appreciation to God for their covenant of life, desire to responsibly practice an all-comprehensive Christian way of life. A biblical Christian way of life includes all of education and does not compromise covenant obligations in learning. Accordingly, a necessary result of God's covenant is Christian schooling.

The belief that God's covenant with His people is the matchless base upon which Christian schools are to be built is not a new concept. Louis Berkhoff has written that:

> Advocates of Christian education have always maintained that the Christian school is an outgrowth of the covenant idea, and is absolutely necessary in order to enable the child to appreciate its covenant privileges and to understand the solemn significance of its baptism in the triune God.[1]

Arnold Brink writes that "The cornerstone of Christian

education then was the gracious covenant between God and man. . . . It is still true that the covenant of God with man is the foundation of Christian education."[2] Cornelius Van Til has defended Christian schools from the covenant perspective. Van Til believes that:

> The final apologetic for Christian education must show that Christian education is involved in the covenant, that the covenant is involved in creation, that creation is involved in the idea of God and that without God man's life and experience would be entirely meaningless.[3]

Accordingly, Christian schools should be established exclusively upon the scriptural covenant of God. Any other ground is untenable. Part I of this book demonstrates the clear-cut scriptural warrant for Christian schools, and that Christians who do not advance Christian schools compromise God's covenant and their obligations to it.

Part II of this book offers a biblical view of the Christian philosophy of education, which is drawn entirely from the scriptural covenant presented in Part I. Key aspects considered are the Creator-creature distinction; man - from within the covenant of redemption and from outside that covenant; the place of the triune God, the Holy Spirit in particular, and the written word of God as they govern Christian education; and the all-comprehensive antithesis between the biblical world view and way of life in contrast to the non-biblical world view and way of life.

Part III presents a teaching-learning process which consistently implements the Christian's covenant responsibilities and philosophy of education. An integrated approach to learning[4] is presented with specific emphasis on individual, student-oriented, curriculum design. This approach, which is significantly different from "traditional Christian education,"[5] is a conscious attempt to root out the remnants of humanism which remain within the teaching-learning process of the Christian school movement. Jay Adams stated "that the Christian school movement is presently unable to achieve its deepest ends and lacks verve and excitement precisely because it is riddled with humanism."[6]

This volume was written to help the Christian school

movement achieve its deepest ends with verve and excitement by understanding God's basic covenant schema as it applies to education.

NOTES

1. Cornelius Jaarsma, Ed. FUNDAMENTALS OF CHRISTIAN EDUCATION THEORY AND PRACTICE (Grand Rapids, Michigan: Eerdmans Publishing Company, 1953), p.20.

2. Arnold Brink *The Foundations of Christian Education* THE CHRISTIAN SCHOOL ANNUAL, 1958, p.132.

3. Cornelius Van Til ESSAYS ON CHRISTIAN EDUCATION (Presbyterian and Reformed Publishing Company, 1974), p.125.

4. Geraldine J. Steensma SHAPING SCHOOL CURRICULUM: INTEGRAL LEARNING FOR CHILDREN: A BIBLICAL VIEW (Grand Rapids, Michigan: Signal Publishing Company, 1984), pp.1-7.

5. A. A. Baker THE SUCCESSFUL CHRISTIAN SCHOOL (Pensacola, Florida: A Beka Book Publications, 1979) pp.42-49.

6. Jay Adams BACK TO THE BLACKBOARD: DESIGN FOR A BIBLICAL CHRISTIAN SCHOOL (Phillipsburg, New Jersey: Presbyterian and Reformed Publishing Company, 1982) p.13.

Introduction

Have you heard about Drew Colfax? Drew is 18 years old and is being actively recruited by Yale, Amherst, Harvard, Haverford and Princeton. No, he is not an athlete with good grades. In fact, Drew has never spent a day in school!

Why is Drew being recruited? There are several reasons. "He is a physicist and builder.... He installed a solar-powered electrical system [in his California home].... An avid stargazer, Drew has written a weekly astronomy column for the local newspaper and built his own telescope from scratch, along with an observatory to put it in. He ground the mirror, accurate to a millionth of an inch, by hand."

A Princeton university spokeswoman said, "'Drew was one of our most extraordinary applicants.... We've never seen a kid like this.... He is truly a thinker. Most kids submit a one-page essay with their applications. Drew gave us five single-spaced, typewritten pages. Not only was it beautifully written, it was quite profound.'"

Drew's education has been at Mountain School. At this unorthodox school, "there are no tests, no grades, no homework. [Students] are encouraged to read - do book reviews - and do projects." They also visit museums, attend concerts and the ballet, and they sit around the table discussing history or reading historical novels. "'We never had to do all the boring, tedious homework people do,'" said Drew.

Mountain School is actually a home school. Drew's parents were "appalled by local schools." Their view "is not so much a critique of education as it is a cultural critique." Drew's father claims that "ninety-four percent of the public schools in this country are not interested in education. You can send your children to a poor school and hope they survive. We simply didn't want to take that chance with our kids."

Incidentally, Drew's older brother also went to Mountain School and is now a "pre-med student in his third year at Harvard, where his grades have been strictly A's and B's."[1]

Most parents cannot home school their children. Few parents are able to and rarely are they willing to carry out the long term commitment required. Most children do not have a sociology professor and a high school English teacher as parents. Christian parents can, however, band together, pool their talents, finances, and ministries, and establish a parent-controlled Christian school.

Not only can Christian students build telescopes, solar-powered electrical systems, and write superior compositions, but they can comprehend with minds that are captive to the obedience of Christ, and with wills that use these things for Christian service. Such is the outpouring of God's grace in a school where God is uniquely at work in the life of each individual student.

NOTES

1. *Colleges Woo Home-Taught Sheep Herder,* THE PLAIN DEALER, May 1, 1986

PART I
God's Covenant - The Biblical Foundation

All of life is religious. In fact, life is religion, and religion in Scripture means covenant with or covenant apart from God. Our covenant with God must not be restricted to the specific covenants made with Moses, Abraham, and Noah. Rather, the horizon of God's promise greatly exceeds any particular covenant revealed in Scripture. God's covenant is the foundational unity that encircles and binds all the acts of humanity and all the relationships of society. It is from the basis of God's covenant with his people that we should understand Christ, and consequently every story in Scripture, as God revealing Himself.

A covenant has been defined as "a contract, or compact, or agreement between parties."[1] In Scripture, a covenant is "a bond in blood, or a bond of life and death, sovereignly administered."[2] It is a commitment of persons, one to another, a pledge to the death, and it represents a loyalty inaugurated by a formal blood-shedding process. The shedding of blood represents the power, strength, and intensity of the covenant relationship initiated by God with His people through Christ Jesus.

In the scriptural covenant, God gave to man a position which lifted the created person to fellowship with Himself. Even after the Fall, when man was unwilling and bound in sin, God gratuitously bound Himself to man again by committing Himself in a covenant of grace to redeem a people to Himself.

> By creation God bound himself to man in covenantal relationship. After man's fall into sin, the God of all creation graciously bound himself to man again by committing himself to redeem a people to himself from lost humanity. From creation to consummation the covenantal bond has determined the relation of God to his people. The extent of the divine covenants reaches from the beginning of the world to the end of the age."[3]

Consequently, man in covenant with the God of Scripture is able through the Holy Spirit to be responsible and faithful to his almighty God.

The covenant relationship which God has established with His people is a total life relationship. It is an all inclusive relationship where "man's obligation to his Maker [extends] to every area of human activity."[4] Clearly, such a covenant obligation to the eternal God, the Creator and Preserver of all should encompass the entire education of God's covenant children. Over and above this, "The children who have been baptized will sense its significance, and those who have not will long for it, provided that they receive God's blessing."[5]

Covenant of Life[6]

The Adamic Administration

God initiates written revelation of Himself to His people by telling us that in the beginning He created the heaven and the earth. With this statement God plainly sets forth a sharp distinction between that which is created and Himself. This is a vital point which must be taught to all God's children. Yet, it is not enough to only tell the children that heaven and earth were created by God. Much more than this must be taught. Once a youngster's heart and mind has been changed by the Spirit of the Lord, "he will also long to hear more; he will want to hear about God living in constant communion with the entire creation."[7] The significance is that Scripture teaches that all things come from God and that man is to direct all things to the glory of God.

Then God said, "Let Us make man in Our image, according to Our likeness and let them rule over all the earth" (Gen 1:26,27). God, in making man and woman in His own image, bound Himself to them and enabled them to live in an active relationship with Himself. Furthermore, God did not intend that the world remain just as He made it. Mankind was created to direct all of creation to God's glory, that is, to form a culture glorifying to the Lord. This constitutes the heart of our active relationship with God. In other words, man was to live in absolute obedience to our holy Lord. In complete submission to God's Word, with grateful acknowledgement of God's goodness, we are to implement Godly dominion over all of creation. Without doubt, this Spirit-directed ministry service is an active relationship with the covenant God of the Bible. It incorporates acquiring knowledge in a supplementary operation through Scripture and the law of God which is innately written on the hearts of students.

Before the Fall, Adam and Eve were immersed from within and without by God's revelation of Himself. There was nothing else that existed. Only God's creation confronted them. Wherever Adam and Eve turned they were face to face with God disclosing Himself to them through His creation. God personally placed Himself before them in and through every act, thought, and relationship. Consequently, before sin entered the world, all that man thought and did was in accord with God's holiness and with God's understanding for man. Whatever man learned or created was fully reflective of God's glory and in complete harmony with His plan and purpose. Adam and Eve were always receiving and producing God-glorifying education. The whole earth was God's school and all mankind was enrolled in Adam their representative. No other system existed save God's school system; a system which always honored and glorified the Lord God as man exercised dominion over the heaven-and-earth curriculum.

The Fall

Satan was alert to the covenant of life that God arranged with Adam. He used the serpent to deceive Eve, and Eve to allure Adam into disobedience to God's command not to eat of the tree in the midst of the garden. Satan lied to Eve. He intentionally misrepresented God's word to Adam, and, thus, God's purpose for mankind. According to Satan, man would "be like God" (Gen 3:5 NIV). In effect, Satan succeeded in getting Adam and Eve to declare themselves free of God, loose of God's control, liberated to establish what is true and what is not true, and to create their own standards. Hence, in sin, mankind believed themselves to be set free or autonomous from God, their Creator and Sustainer. As a result, mankind has believed that the world is a world where God is not God, and that in this world man is the highest authority. Satan in triumph misleads all the thinking and acting of mankind by shedding a false light on all things, and now, in total depravity, mankind autonomously interprets all things falsely.

The Fall of Adam and Eve into sin marks the origin of godless education. Once the Covenant of Life was broken by them, mankind was no longer able to rightly "think God's thoughts after Him [or to know that] education is implication into God's interpretation."[8] Rather, education, no longer Godly, became characterized by the same traits as the Fall of man into sin. God's school system was exchanged for an educational system which declares itself to be free of God, outside God's control, and able to establish its own standards. God could no longer determine the curriculum for the classroom. The Creator was disbarred from the minds of children, and the Lord's glory was abandoned in favor of the glory of man. The school system which was established apart from God's Covenant of Life is actually a covenant with Satan and death. This covenant with Satan is actively pursued and practiced today in all educational systems where the God of Scripture is not continuously held in highest regard.

Covenant of Grace

According to Adam's vantage point, the gulf between himself and his Creator was unbridgeable. God's righteousness and holiness had been violated. His justice had to be satisfied by the eternal death of Adam and thus all mankind. Nevertheless, God sought out Adam in the garden. God, in an act of absolute grace, exhibited His mercy and goodness to Adam and a people He would call to Himself through a promise to deliver them from sin and eternal death. This means that Adam and men of God are duty bound to "faith and repentance, worship and obedience, separation from the world and consecration to God."[9] On the other hand, God granted reconciliation and communion with himself in everlasting life, but after the Fall, man had to live by faith alone; faith in God's promise or faith in himself.

Faith in God's promise to deliver a people for Himself from sin and eternal death is vital to education. Education according to God's promise means that Godly students and teachers will dutifully express their faith in the Word of God, their repentance from sin, their worship of Almighty God, their obedience to God's law, their separation from iniquity, and, thus, consecrate all of their life to God. Only schools which honor God's promise can guide and instruct students toward their allegiance to God their Creator. Parents who wish to fully perform their covenant-calling are obligated, in every respect, to support God-exalting schools or to acknowledge compromise. Godly parents are to provide Biblical education for the children of Christ's inheritance. This education must be according to faith in God's promise or it will be based on faith in human autonomy.

On the occasion of the birth of Cain, Adam said, "I have gotten a man from the Lord" (Gen 4:1). Thus, Adam and Eve acknowledged the Lordship of Almighty God over their children, and perhaps they understood that the new life before them was a sign from God of the promise of life which He had given. Surely they told their children about God's grace and promise of deliverance. They must have prayed for their children to affirm faith in God's grace. This is always a principal concern of Godly parents. Nevertheless, Cain rejected the promise. He did not give his heart and life to the Lord as did Abel, his brother. Instead, Cain "went out from the presence of the Lord" (Gen 4:16) to live for himself.

Parents who declare faith in the promise of the Lord also avow that all their children are a gift from the Lord, a sign of His promise of life. They seek for God's grace to be extended in faith to their children that they might not go out from the presence of the Lord. Yet many of these believing parents enroll their children of the Lord's inheritance in schools where the presence of the Lord is ignored, denied or otherwise defamed. Schools where children are taught to live lives as unto themselves are not in harmony with the Lord's promise of grace. Parents who entrust their children to these schools jeopardize their right to some of God's blessings.

* * * * *

"God saw that the wickedness of man was great in the earth, and that every imagination of the thoughts of his heart was only evil continuously. . . . But Noah found grace in the eyes of the Lord. . . . Noah was a just man and Noah walked with God" (Gen 6:5,8,9). Apart from the grace of God given to Noah, the line of demarcation between Seth and Cain was obliterated into one evil culture. Noah stood as the one man from all mankind in whom Christ's Spirit, the promised Redeemer, worked. Through the seed of this one man God promised to redeem a particular people unto Himself. Evil must die. The corruption of the world went face to face with God through His servant Noah and perished. Noah stood firmly rooted in the covenant which God established with him. "Thus did Noah; according to all that God commanded him, so did he" (Gen 6:22). By obediently ordering his life according to the revealed will of God, Noah was saved. For the sake of the coming Redeemer, Noah was saved and through this the Lord gave us new life.

Our new life is also a covenant life with God. This life, like Noah's, is to be in total contrast to continuous evil. We need to teach our covenant children about God's wrath, evil culture, and the unceasing corruption of the world. This corruption includes secularist education where God's particular grace is renounced in either an overt or covert fashion. Educators who have found grace in the Lord and who are just and who walk with God will set themselves apart. They will stand in covenant with the Lord as Noah and do all that God commands. Only schools which accept the authority of Almighty God can provide an education which orders life according to the revealed will of God. They will build a culture and school system according to the Word of God as Noah built an ark according to the Word of God. Only in perfect submission to the authority of the Word of God and the power of God can students learn righteousness, learn love for the Redeemer, and learn loyalty to God's covenant. God's covenant schools cheerfully acknowledge all of this, while schools who stand on their own authority are anathema to Him.

* * * * *

Adam, Noah, and all men after them must learn to desire the Redeemer. It is only through Him that mankind can again enjoy communion with God. Yet, in the land of Shinar, all of the people on earth rejected faith in the Redeemer by going their own way. In denying the covenant God, they attempted to build "a city and a tower, whose top may reach unto heaven" (Gen 11:4). This is also the goal of godless education. Accordingly, educators who live apart from communion with God attempt through acquired learning to build a city and a tower unto the honor and glory of mankind. They want to reach unto heaven without the Redeemer, without faith, and without repentance from godless living. In sharp contrast, our view is that a covenant relationship with the Redeemer is a prerequisite for

Godly learning. Clearly, God despises Godless men, and thus despises educators or educational systems which build a life and culture apart from His covenant and their Godly responsibilities.

* * * * *

Although Abram had no righteousness or worthiness of his own, God came to him and established His covenant with him. God called Abram out to set him and his seed apart. God revealed through Abram that a contrast between the life of faith and the life of the flesh had to be vividly set forth if the covenant life was not to be destroyed by the religious life of the flesh. God's chosen people were set apart in order that they might understand that faith in the Redeemer required breaking with idolatry. When Pharaoh was stopped by God from taking Abram's wife, it was not their marriage which was primarily at stake. It was the promised seed, the Redeemer, whose life was threatened and protected. So it is when believing parents threaten the covenant which God has made with them by enrolling their children in idolatrous schools. They follow Abram by jeopardizing their covenant inheritance because they fail to set apart their seed by condescending to educate their children in schools that teach according to the religious life of the flesh. On the other hand, believing parents are to join with Abram as symbols of an entirely new life, a whole, new, covenant community. Like the coming Redeemer, who dwells apart from all that is sin, believers are to educate their children apart from ungodliness and idolatry.

More is revealed about Abram being set apart when he declines all gifts offered by the King of Sodom (Gen 14:20). Abram had declared to the Lord God Most High that he would not receive any favors or material things from the Canaanites because he did not want to be considered one of them, or become dependent upon them. He refused to befriend them, to live with them, or to join in life with them. Rather, Abram looked to the Lord God to bless him lest the Lord be robbed of His rightful place and full glory by the blasphemous boasting of the Canaanites (Gen 14:22-23). Believing parents must also decline educational gifts offered by unbelieving educators, "free" public education. These gifts and favors are not given with the proper recognition of the rightful place and glory of the Lord God Most High, and are therefore blasphemous forms of learning.

Schooling which rightly praises the Creator and Redeemer God is not entangled with godlessness.

Being totally and uncompromisingly separated unto the Lord, in short, is God's covenant with Abram. As God further unfolds revelation about Himself and His relationship with Abram, henceforth renamed Abraham, God says, "I am the Almighty God; walk before Me, and be blameless" (Gen 17:1). As Abraham's seed, believers and their seed are also to adhere to what God said to Abraham in "everlasting covenant" (Gen 17:7). Yet, Lot failed to stand apart and be blameless when abiding in Sodom. Peter writes that righteous Lot was "vexed with the filthy manner of life of the wicked" (II Pet. 2:7). This is because Lot, although undoubtedly a believer, did not break from the sinful ways of these evil people. Rather, he sat at the gate of Sodom. He tolerated the engagement of his daughters to Sodomites and lingered even after God's angels exhorted him to leave Sodom. Consequently, even after the Lord rained brimstone and fire upon Sodom and Gomorrah, the minds of his wife and daughters remained infiltrated with paganism. Lot's wife looked back toward this wickedness and was consumed while his daughters greatly sinned by bearing their father's sons. So it came to pass that Lot was saved, but his descendants were lost.

Believing parents who enroll the Lord's children in secular schools, where sin is exceedingly grave, are like Lot living in Sodom. They are not blameless when they vex their children with the filthy manner of education of the wicked and fail to separate from the sinful ways of godless educators. These parents tolerate the educational engagements and entanglements with the sons of perdition and falter even after the Word of God exhorts them to "keep my covenant" (Gen 17:9). As a result, just as Lot's descendants were allowed to slip into paganism, the posterity of these believing parents may also be lost.

The covenant revelation continues with God directing Abraham to sacrifice Isaac. At the conclusion of Abraham's test to offer Isaac, The Lord said, "because thou hast done this thing, and hast not withheld thy son, thine only son. . . because thou hast obeyed my voice" (Gen 22:16,18). I will bless thee. Godly parents must also follow Abraham's example and not withhold their sons and daughters from the ways of the Lord. Only schools which acknowledge absolute submission to the Lord are free from the guilt of withholding the truth from their children's minds.The learning advanced in godly schools is unique and in complete contrast to other schools because they alone obey the voice of Almighty God. Clearly, God promises to bless believing parents and their seed when they obey Him by educating their children according to all of His commands - which are the educational standards for all time.

* * * * *

Jacob stands in opposition to Esau because he heartily pursued the inheritance of the promise while Esau had contempt for the promise and the Redeemer. Esau did not bow to the Lord. He attempted in pride to live according to his own strength, and in fact sold his birthright, assuming that he could succeed in life without God's blessing. Furthermore, he took unto himself two Hittite women as his wives, because he disregarded the promises of God. On the other hand, Jacob, with Rebekah, mixed faith and sin together in order to gain for himself the blessing of God. Many believing parents also mix faith and sin when educating their children. They rightly seek the blessing of the Lord but compromise with schools and educators who teach solely upon their own strength and assume that truth can be learned and lived while holding the Redeemer in contempt. Certainly the Lord does not sell His blessing as Jacob thought, nor does He educate His covenant children through teachers and schools which disregard our Creator God. Education which holds firm to the Lord and His covenant has no room for compromise.

God's covenant foundations for education are seen in other aspects of Jacob's life. When he flees Laban, we find that "Rachel had stolen the images that were her father's" (Gen 31:19). She took them because she had not fully given her heart to the Lord but retained hope that another son could be born through the aid of the idols. Engaging covenant children in a godless education system and hoping that as learners the students will bear the truth is like Rachel hoping that idols will cause her to bear children. Instead, covenant learners should wrestle with God like Jacob in order to be given the blessing of true learning. Our children must understand that our struggle for the blessing of true learning is not with men, but with the God of Israel. They must cling solely to the Lord for His covenant promise. Only in the power of the Lord can they prevail to receive the blessing of education in the Truth.

* * * * *

When the Covenant of Grace is further revealed at Sinai, God expands the covenant administration from family caretaking to the context of a whole covenant people or an entire covenant community. This expansion reveals further the covenant foundation for education.

* * * * *

The Lord God Almighty, JEHOVAH, said to Moses, "I have remembered My covenant" (Ex 6:5). Thus, Moses did as the Lord commanded and repeatedly went to Pharaoh to mediate for the Israelites. In this way, Moses was a foreshadowing of the coming Redeemer who would mediate God's covenant on behalf of His particular people. But unlike the Redeemer God, Moses objected when Pharaoh made circumstances tough. Moses believed that his lack of eloquent speech was the cause of his failure to persuade Pharaoh to let the Israelites go, as if his success was dependent on polished exhortation rather than the revealed Word of God. Pharaoh did not believe or obey the Lord. In spite of the fact that the ten plagues only affected Egypt and not Israel, Pharaoh did not have faith through which to see that the Lord deals with His people differently from those who do not believe in Him.

Unbelieving educators and their school systems are like Pharaoh with his lack of faith and hard heart. They do not understand that the Lord teaches, guides, directs, motivates, and commands His people differently from those who do not believe in Him. The antithesis is all-comprehensive. Godly parents know that the mediatory work of the Redeemer is essential for covenant students to rightly interpret the universe by the revealed Word of God. Ungodly educators say with Pharaoh, "Who is the Lord that I should obey His voice. . . . I do not know the Lord" (Ex 5:2). Therefore they reject the true interpretation of the universe and exchange Godly education for unrighteousness. Why do some covenant parents suppress the all-encompassing distinction between the way God educates within His covenant schools from the way students are educated in school systems that do not know or uphold the Lord? Could the answer be that "it requires discarding . . . [a great myth] that props up the whole edifice [public schools]: that all men are created equal and that government, as the great equalizer, is the most benevolent dispenser of human goodness, generosity, and justice on earth."[10]

* * * * *

Upholding God's covenant promises, Caleb reported back to Moses saying, "Let us go up at once, and possess [the land]"; (Num 13:30). But the other spies said, "We are not able to go up against the people; for they are stronger than we" (Num 13:31). Caleb's faithful report was rejected! The Israelites failed to believe, in faith, when Joshua and Caleb declared that "If the Lord delight in us, then He will bring us into this land. . . . Only rebel not ye against the Lord, neither fear ye the people of the land. . . . The Lord is with us: fear them not" (Num 14:8,9). So it was that a generation of Israelites died in the desert because they thought Canaan was nothing more than a land flowing with milk and honey. They did not recognize that entering the land meant fellowship with the Lord God through the promised Redeemer.

Correspondingly, many Godly leaders, educators and parents do not recognize that learning at Godly schools means fellowship with the Lord God through the promised Redeemer. Rather than go up against the giant public school systems or the secularist state boards of education, because they appear to be more powerful, better equipped and well financed, these individuals rebel against the Lord. As a result, many covenant children in every generation have been lost in the godless desert of secular education. On the other hand, covenant honoring schools are much more than the milk of Scripture courses and the honey of prayer. They are schools which facilitate learning and a life of living in allegiance to Almighty God. Alone they stand, honoring the Lord by instructing students to interpret all of life and all facts from God's perspective rather than to evaluate by size or social status.

* * * * *

"Then the Lord spoke to Moses and Aaron at Mount Hor . . . saying, Aaron shall be gathered to his people; for he shall not enter the land which I have given to the sons of Israel, because you rebelled against My word" (Num 20:23,24). Aaron, whom compromising Christian educators and parents symbolize, wanted to be self-sufficient in his own right. This resulted in condemnation and death for Aaron. Compromising Christian educators and parents too, will be condemned because of rebellion against God. Self-sufficiency in man is cursed and vigorously denounced by God, for only the sovereign God of Scripture is self-sufficient. Aaron could no more fetch water out of the rock under his own command than can secular educators interpret the world correctly and teach the truth. Truth originates in and is revealed exclusively by the Lord God.

* * * * *

At the time of Joshua's death, Scripture says "Israel served the Lord all the days of Joshua, and all the days of the elders who outlived Joshua" (Jos 24:31). Just before he died, Joshua called for all Israel to give them a final address. He began by rightly acknowledging the Lord God for having fought for them in accord with His covenant. Accordingly, Joshua instructed them "to keep and to do all that is written in the book of the Law of Moses, that ye turn not aside therefrom to the right hand or to the left; [in order that you may not associate with these nations] ... cleave unto the Lord [and] love the Lord" (Jos 23:6-8). Then the Lord shall bring to pass, said Joshua, all good things which the Lord your God promised. ... But when you transgress the covenant of the Lord your God, which He commanded you, and go and serve other gods, ... then the anger of the Lord will burn against you (Jos 23:14,16). Therefore he concluded that they should serve the Lord in sincerity and truth! They should choose whom they would serve, the Lord or the gods of Egypt.

The choice which Joshua offered was a complete antithesis, and it is the same choice which confronts educators today. Educators cannot serve two masters; they must serve the Creator God of Scripture or other gods. They must do all that is written in the book of the Law or transgress the covenant of the Lord. Then they will receive all the good things God promised or receive the anger of the Lord. "Can one intelligently assume that he is both a creature and not a creature, a sinner and not a sinner? Can any one intelligently assume ... that God is the source of possibility, and ... that possibility is the source of God?"[11] Can one uphold the claims of Christianity while enrolling their children in schools run by Hitler, Gadhafi, Stalin or Mao? Would the Israelites have enrolled their children in Philistine schools? Joshua would not, and neither should contemporary Christians send the children God has placed under their care to statist public schools. It causes the anger of the Lord to burn.

Believing educators and students are not to turn to the right or to the left of God's covenant laws. They are to cleave to the Lord and to love the Lord throughout all of their days. This includes all of their education, which cannot be restricted to the sabbath. On the other hand, Godly educators and students are not to come among false educators who serve and bow down to other gods. These false educators are to be driven away by the Lord through His educators lest they become "snares," and "traps," and "scourges," and "thorns" (Jos 23:12-13). Why is it then that many believing educators, parents and students are engaged or married to unbelieving educators and their school systems? Surely the Lord has taught us, through His servant, Joshua, to say but for me and my children and my school, we will serve the Lord (Jos 24:15). The Lord is everything in education and to His people, or He is nothing (Jos 22:5).

* * * * *

In the book of Judges, the Lord God said, "I will never break My covenant with you, and as for you," you shall make no covenant with the inhabitants of this land; you shall tear down their altars. But you have not obeyed My voice. Why have you done this? (Jud 2:1,2). Similarly, the Lord has said to believing educators and parents of covenant children that He will never break His covenant with them, and that they shall not make covenants with secular educators; they are to tear down the secular altars of humanism. But many believers have not obeyed the voice of the Lord. Without doubt:

> [T]he Lord calls His people to engage in unceasing spiritual warfare [for the minds, hearts, and souls of children in their schooling] against anything and everything that opposes the honor of His name. For us today it would be just as sinful and disobedient to enter into a spiritual agreement [to cooperatively educate covenant children in concert with unbelieving educators], to live in peace with the forces of unbelief [in academic peace with unbelieving secular

educators], as it was for Israel to make an alliance with the Canaanites.[12]

"Why have believers done this?" (Jud 2:2 NIV) asks the Lord. It is because of unbelief. With unbelief in their hearts, the Israelites halted their war against the Canaanites, and this same unbelief in the hearts of Godly educators halted their war against humanistic education. Furthermore, the Israelites associated with the Canaanites more and more. As a result, the Israelites no longer looked upon the Canaanites as their enemies, but allowed the worship of Baal to penetrate deeply into their way of life.[13] In the twentieth century, many children of the covenant have been educated by the secular humanists. As a result, they no longer look upon the humanistic educators and materialists as their enemies, but have learned to welcome their counseling, life-style, and materialistic values with a sugar coating of Godly atmosphere. It follows that God is distant and does not give His full covenant communion to these educators and parents or their seed.

* * * * *

After the Israelites requested a king, which revealed their lack of trust in the Lord, they lost a battle to the Philistines and allowed them to capture the ark of God. The Philistines took the ark of God and placed it next to their god, Dagon, but twice Dagon fell face down before the ark of the Lord. At first, when Dagon fell down, the Philistines attributed this to chance. However, the next night the Lord destroyed Dagon and in short order the Philistines realized that "the hand of the Lord was heavy upon them" (I Sam 5:7).

Secular educators are like the Philistines because they ultimately ascribe the cause of all events to the god of chance. Sometimes believing educators also are like the Philistines. They stand the Creator God up against the secular theory of evolution as if the two can stand together before the bar of human evaluation or verification. This degradation of the Creator submits the Lord to the limits of probabilities or possibilities. Education that is Godly and scriptural is never limited to or dependent upon the foundation of chance. When education is founded upon God's covenant, educators will always submit learning which corresponds with logic, reason, statistics, and chance to the authority of Scripture. Without this submission in all of education, the Lord God is blasphemed, and all subsequent learning is false.

* * * * *

Samuel confronted Saul saying, "Thou hast done foolishly: thou hast not kept the commandment of the Lord thy God" (I Sam 13:13). Therefore the Lord turned from Saul for not fully trusting in the Lord in all things. Saul turned to his own means. Although he felt the pressure of an emergency battle with the Philistines, it was not an excuse to void the Lord's command. Saul's disobedient sacrifice resulted in both he and his family being out of accord with God's covenant and as a result, the Lord "sought out for Himself a man after His own heart" (I Sam 13:14).

The Space Age has not changed God. He continues to seek out for Himself a particular people after His own heart. Yet, it can hardly be said that teachers and students are effectively seeking the heart of the Lord with all their heart, mind, soul, and strength while engaged in a secular school system which does not trust the Lord in anything! Covenant children cannot be expected to seek out the heart of God when their teachers do not know the heart of God. Unbelieving educators will direct covenant students away from the Lord's heart because they know no other direction. And, according to John Goodlad, this influence is formative. He claims that "the intellectual terrain is laid out by the teacher. The paths for walking through it are largely predetermined by the teacher."[14] Accordingly, when believing parents enroll their children in secular schools, to be largely taught by unbelieving teachers, they should not expect them to learn to keep the commandments of the Lord. This will be the result because they have been taught to ignore God's commands under all circumstances, and not just when under the felt pressure of an emergency.

* * * * *

"Then David said to the Philistines, thou comest to me with a sword, and with a spear, and with a shield; but I come to thee in the name of the Lord of hosts, the God of the armies of Israel, whom thou hast defied" (I Sam 17:45). He knew the Lord's power and had submitted fully to it when he previously slew the bear and the lion. On the other hand, Goliath, the unbeliever, relied on his own strength and size and upon his own gods. He thought it a disgrace to surrender to the God of Abraham, Isaac, and Jacob, and the Law given to Israel by God's servant Moses. In contrast, David knew it was not his skill with the sling which defeated the giant Philistine; he recognized that the victory came by the power of the Lord.

Godly educators also know, like David, that genuine learning victories come by the power of the Lord. Certainly teaching skills and methods, curriculum and other materials are important to the teaching-learning process, as the sling was to David's victory. But in reality, it is the Lord's grace which ultimately causes true learning. Unbelieving educators reject this grace as an unnecessary addition to the teaching-learning process. These educators rely wholly upon their own power to manipulate the minds of learners by using the most expensive equipment and modern techniques available while all the time defiling the power of God. God's educators and parents know that expensive equipment and modern techniques and new school buildings are as useless as Goliath's armor and spear if they are pitted against the power of God. They know that complete submission to God's power is absolutely essential if education is to produce learning victories in the minds of covenant students.

* * * * *

Absalom flattered the people of Israel and turned them away from God's covenant. He "stole the hearts of the men of Israel" (II Sam 15:6) with blarney, and led them away from David, the Lord's anointed, in rebellion. The rebellion failed, but David was not immediately restored to his kingdom. The representative head of God's covenant and God's Redeemer, the man who had delivered them from the Philistines and who symbolized the eternal Deliverer, was subjected to a debate of the advantages and disadvantages of his kingship. Although David, in his grief for Absalom, erroneously let his feeling rather than God's calling direct him, the people had no excuse for failing to act according to their covenant obligations by promptly reinstating David as king.

Contemporary believers often debate the advantages and disadvantages of enrolling their children in either secular schools or schools which seek to educate according to God's covenant bond. Such debates cannot be used as the basis for the existence of God's schools or for establishing enrollment rationale. Furthermore, covenant obligations are not open to discussion. Moses wrote,

> What doth the Lord thy God require of thee, but to fear the Lord thy God, to walk in all His ways, and to love Him, and to serve the Lord thy God with all thy heart and with all thy soul, to keep the commandments of the Lord, and His statutes, which I will command thee this day for thy good? (Deut 10:12,13).

These responsibilities must not be compromised by debate, nor can they be satisfied in a secular school system where believers must bridle them or where unbelievers continuously malign them. Such accommodation is flattery to unbelievers who in rebellion steal the hearts and minds of covenant learners. Secular schooling is rebellion because it educates apart from the fear of God. It teaches that it is not necessary to learn to walk in all of the Lord's ways. Nor is it imperative to the secular educator to love the Lord with all the teaching-learning process, to serve the Lord God with all learning and in every activity of life, to keep the commandments of the Lord, and to uphold His statutes. God is not pleased with this type of schooling. Only schools which are founded upon God's covenant can be used to satisfy the believer's covenant obligations in education.

* * * * *

Solomon's wisdom was not due to cleverness, piousness, or diligent study. Rather, "all Israel . . . saw that the wisdom of God was in him, to do justice" (I Kings 3:28). Accordingly, as a young king, Solomon lived in covenant communion with the Lord, and this enabled him and the Israelites to have the world and all life opened up to them. But later this was closed because Solomon and the people were unfaithful and willfully rejected the Lord's covenant and His statutes. Thus, the Lord rent the Kingdom away from him.

Godly educators know that an education apart from the wisdom of God is a violation of the Lord's covenant. These educators desire that covenant students demonstrate a wisdom which is clearly the wisdom of God, and a covenant communion life which is wholly in harmony with all of the Lord's commands. These educational goals please the Lord as Solomon's prayer for wisdom pleased Him. The Lord was gratified because Solomon did not selfishly ask for long life, neither did he desire materialistic riches, nor did he ask for power over the lives of other people - all primary career ambitions of a secularist society. Long life, riches, and power over the lives of other people can only honor the Lord when just servants of God walk in the ways of the Lord's commandments. This walk is the primary goal of Godly schools and Godly educators for the lives of covenant students. Secularist institutions are not righteous. They do not understand and they do not seek after God in any of their educational practices. Certainly God is pleased when believing parents seek the wisdom of God for their children in schools which willfully walk in the straight and narrow way.

* * * * *

Evil in Israel continued to wax greater and greater. King Ahab "did evil in the sight of the Lord above all who were before him" (I Kings 16:30). In complete rejection of the Lord, "he went and served Baal, and worshipped him" (I Kings 16:31). He led the people in deifying and worshipping the forces of nature. In response to this evil, through the prophet Elijah, God withdrew His Word by hiding Elijah. After three years of drought, the glory of the Lord came forth out of concealment on Mount Carmel. There the God of the covenant confronted Baal. Until they saw the fire of the Lord consume Elijah's sacrifice, the people thought one of two possible opinions were valid worship: worship of the covenant God our Creator or worship of the genius of man. Yet, even after the power of the Lord was clearly revealed, rather than surrendering to the Lord God, Ahab persevered in evil ways by following the counsel of Jezebel instead of the Word of God.

Secular education is likewise moving further away from the covenant God, and its evil is growing. This education completely rejects the Lord because it has deified nature and science by worshipping the created rather than the Creator. Horace Mann, often considered the founder of public schools, chose this course by worshipping the laws of nature. Such unbelieving educators have not retained the Lord God in their worship or their knowledge, so like Baal worshippers, God has given them over to reprobate minds. Furthermore these unbelieving educators have exchanged the truth of God for a lie and in doing so are like the prophets of Baal in influencing God's people away from God for the education of covenant children. To some of God's people it seems as if there may be two possible opinions on what is valid education: Christian and secular. Such believing parents and educators profess themselves to be wise. In reality, they are foolish if they attempt to validate secular education by sprinkling child evangelism on an institution that does not submit to the God of Elijah. Godly academic education builds a separate altar to the Holy God of the Bible where biblical truth is uncompromisingly proclaimed as true. Believing educators in secular institutions cannot withhold from students "that which may be known of God," (Rom 1:19) and also be free of compromise. These believers are teachers in the academic sense of the word but not biblical teachers in the *full* sense of the word. Biblical Christian teachers do not, at any time, withhold biblical teachings from their students. They are, at best, evangelists or biblical moralists who do not purpose to glorify God with Christian education, but seek to save lost souls or to combat the influence of sin while serving God as missionaries in public schools.

Could it be that God is directing the withdrawal of covenant students from public schools and into Christian schools because of their great evil of neglecting Him just as He directed Elijah to withdraw from Ahab? Are Christian schools His way of coming out of concealment to proclaim Christ's command to "teach all nations . . . to observe all things whatsoever I have commanded you" (Matt 28:19,20)?

* * * * *

While in Israel Ahab sold "himself to work wickedness in the sight of the Lord" (I Kings 21:25), Jehosaphat ruled Judah with a heart that "was lifted up in the ways of the Lord" (II Chr 17:6) for he walked according to the Lord's commandments. Jehosaphat not only led Judah in the worship of the Lord but also proclaimed that the law of God was to rule every area of life. He instructed the princes "to teach in the cities of Judah [with the] book of the law of the Lord" (II Chr 17:7,9). He set an excellent example by preparing his heart to seek after God. When threatened with invasion, Jehosaphat did "seek the Lord"

(II Chr 19:3) with prayer as he stood before the congregation in the house of the Lord. He acknowledged the rule of the Lord God "over all kingdoms" and His "power" and His "might"; he "fell before the Lord, worshiping the Lord" and "stood up to praise the Lord God of Israel with a loud voice on high" (II Chr 20:6,18).

In sharp contrast to Ahab, who is an example of unbelieving educators, Jehosaphat is a Godly example who illustrates education that is in keeping with God's covenant ordinances. Godly education extends the Scriptural principles of Jehosaphat's life to be part of its educational goals. Accordingly, Godly schools teach students to have hearts which lift up the ways of the Lord, to live lives which exemplify the Lord's commandments, to proclaim the Scriptural law of God as the authoritative standard for every area of life, to teach the book of the law of the Lord, to provide an example and guidance for seeking the Lord with prayer, praise and worship, and to uphold the sovereign rule of the Lord God over all the kingdoms of the nations.

Ungodly parents, educators, and institutions do not embrace the above goals, which are imperative if education is to be in harmony with the Lord God and His covenant. It appears, says H. Richard Niebuhr, that "new perplexities arise as devoted believers seem to make common cause with secularists, calling, for instance, for the elimination of religion from public education."[15] Why do believing educators not see "what is often meant [by secular educators] is that not only the claims of religious groups but all consideration of the claims of Christ and God should be banished from the spheres of [education] where other gods, called values, reign."[16] Secular educators are like Ahab who sold himself to do wickedness by substituting Baal for the Lord God because they, too, substitute the false gods of reason, science, and humanity for the Lord God. Moreover, many believing educators fail to follow Jehosaphat in that they accommodate secular educators rather than clearly expound the full counsel of God's Word.

* * * * *

While Israel and Judah were separated there was much evil among the kings and their people. Athaliah murdered her own grandchildren, the king of Syria was bribed with temple treasures, idol worship continued, and several kings were assassinated. Even the kings who "did that which was right in the sight of the Lord" (II Cor 20:32.33) failed to follow the Lord's command to remove the pagan high places of worship. Hatred of the covenant and of the living God grew to the point that the Word of God became a burden. In both Israel and Judah "the heathen idea here prevails that the gods are subject to the kings, that their help is at the kings' disposal as long as the kings honor them."[17]

In Judah, King Ahaz reigned "and did not that which was right in the sight of the Lord his God" (II Kings 16:2). He rejected the covenant God of David and built a new altar fashioned after the altar in Damascus. Ahaz had forsaken the Lord God "and made also melted and cast images of Baalim . . . and burned his children in the fire" (II Chr 28:2,3). Judah now appeared like the land of Canaan before Joshua had been used by the Lord to drive out the Canaanites. The promised land of the Lord God did not look different from other heathen countries. Even in time of trouble, Ahaz rejected the Lord's help. The Lord spoke to Ahaz and unveiled to him the name, Immanuel, the name of the coming Redeemer, the name which affirmed that in the covenant God is with us. Ahaz preferred the gods of Assyria, saying "'I sacrifice to them that they may help me.' But they were the ruin of him, and of all Israel" (II Chr. 28:23).

Jesus says that an educator cannot "serve two masters: for either he will hate the one, and love the other; or else hold to the one, and despise the other" (Matt 6:24). As long as Christian schools and educators are separated from the Lord God, there is great evil in education. Unbelieving educators have an all-comprehensive hatred toward the living God and His Word. These educators claim to be secular because the Word of God is a burden to them. Rather than submit to the Lord of Scripture, they are like the heathens of old who fashion an educational system with the gods of reason, science and humanity, who honor these gods and sacrifice to them, and who are commanded by them. This type of education is evil in the sight of the Lord God and godly people should not dishonor God by participating in it.

Unbelieving educators have forsaken the covenant God and in His stead have built a new educational system which is idolatry to the Lord. Unfortunately, many believing parents and educators have failed to understand that education according to God's covenant is completely different from all other educational systems. Therefore, they either accommodate with secularism by enrolling their children in secular schools, or they start schools in the name of the God of Scripture but build and fashion and pattern them after the secular system. Accommodation with secular education is similar to Ahaz sacrificing his children at the altar of Baalim! Christian schools and educational systems who pattern themselves in the fashion of secular education fail to free themselves from the roots and tentacles of humanism. This is a most common and serious problem for schools which seek to honor God.

Uncompromising Christian parents and educators are striving to build an educational system which is worthy of the Lord. Such a system will not be like secular education. As Israel was to be entirely different from the land of Canaan and the Israelites totally free from the paganism of the Canaanites, God's schools and all their educational practices are to be entirely different from the life and practices of secular schools. While the two types of schools may *appear* similar or the teaching methods *seem* to be the same, in essence they are diametrically different because Christ reigns in the Christian school. God's schools are enmeshed in an unbreakable interlock with Immanuel. Through this covenant, by way of the Redeemer, the Lord God is with us, with each student and each educator throughout the entire learning process. Moreover, the Lord God Almighty has set the educational standards through His Word and in His Word directed His covenant people to worship Him with all of their hearts, souls, minds, and strength. This kind of worship cannot be accomplished while accommodating secular educators nor by building an educational system which is patterned in the fashion of unbelief. Yet it seems that some believers would follow Ahaz and prefer secularism just as he preferred Assyria. Rather than follow the Lord, they trespass against Him by looking for help or education from unbelievers. It is clearly stated that this will bring ruin: "The way of the ungodly shall perish" (Psa 1:6).

* * * * *

"The Lord stirred up the spirit of Cyrus, King of Persia," (Ezra 1:1) to permit the Jews to return from captivity to Jerusalem. However, not all the Jews chose to return. Rather than return to the land of milk and honey, the place of fellowship with the living covenant God, some Jews remained in exile and thus were demonstrating that they lived out of harmony with the Lord. These Jews had learned to enjoy their captors and delighted in their new homes. They would sooner violate their covenant obligations by intermarrying with heathen families than return to the grace of the Lord God and His law for holy living. In addition, the wealthy Jews chose to build beautiful homes while claiming "that the times were not favorable for rebuilding the Lord's house."[18]

The Lord has stirred up the spirits of many of His people to honor their covenant responsibility by building God-glorifying schools. However, not all believers have embraced this return to God-honoring schools. Instead, many believing educators and parents of covenant children remain at home in unbelieving secular schools. They seem to enjoy being captivated by their statist enemies. As in the old intermarriages of Ezra's day, they covenant with unbelievers to carry out their dominion educational obligations for God's family. These believing educators in the modern secular educational arena fail to do as Ezra of old. They do not "make a covenant with our God to put away ... those who tremble at the commandment of our God; and [do not] let [education] be done according to the law" (Ezra 10:3). Rather, excuses are echoed that the times are not favorable, or the costs are too high, or the salaries are too low, or the sacrifice is too great to build God's school system. Yet, at many of these believers' homes, there are two cars, three televisions, complete stereo systems, V.C.R.'s, and computer games; in addition, four week vacations that routinely include recreational swimming, golf, collecting, travelling, and shopping madness are indicative of the unwillingness of some believing educators to make a clean break with the devils of humanism, materialism, socialism and statism.

Accordingly, with Ezra, covenant honoring educators and parents should "make confession unto the Lord God of our fathers, and do His will; and separate yourselves from the people of the land," (Ezra 10:11) from yoking with secular unbelievers. We should say with the Jews to Ezra, "That's right! As you have said, so it is our duty to do" (Ezra 10:12). Our duty to always honor God's covenant, in education and in all of life, is known as radical obedience. Niebuhr says, "obedience is radical when the whole man is involved, so that 'he is not only *doing* something obediently but *is* essentially obedient,' and when he confronts an either-or so that he no longer seeks a neutral position but accepts the burden of decision between good and evil."[19] Clearly, the Lord God Almighty demands radical obedience to His covenant law and statutes. Any educational system which does not stubbornly affirm the Lord God and His covenant are without a Redeemer and are evil. Retreat into pockets of mythical neutrality or behind masks of doing something obediently does not change the fact that education apart from the Lord God is sin. Some Christians evangelizing in public schools attempt to infuse biblical morals into this system. Obedience to biblical morals is nice but it is a false promotion of moral neutrality if the biblical basis is not fully taught as true. Covenant children long for full revelation of the Lord's grace in their classrooms. Furthermore, if the curriculum design and the entire teaching-learning process in Christian schools are not radically biblical, then, humanism has infiltrated our schools by using the Trojan Horse of neutrality.

Christian schools have come to God's covenant army as indispensable equipment for the march. "Many converts curse a faith so exacting that no pagan impulses were safe from its challenge. When the challenge of Christianity [Christian education] slackens, paganism immediately creeps in."[20]

Covenant of Redemption

The Covenant of Grace is part of the Covenant of Redemption and cannot be separated from it, because the Covenant of Grace is the actualization of the Covenant of Redemption.[21] In other words, the goodness of God is extended to humanity in the everyday events or activities of the world by God's common grace. This active grace is made specific and eternal by the removal of sin through redemption which the Lord Jesus Christ, our Redeemer, has granted to His particular people.

The promised Redeemer is Jesus Christ the Mediator. In accord with the covenant, God chose and ordained Christ, His only begotten Son, to be the mediator between God and man. Christ is the full revelation of the promise of salvation for "the elect based on the covenant of redemption that was transacted in eternity between the Father and the Son; and it is solely through the grace conveyed by this covenant that all the descendants of fallen Adam who have been saved have obtained life."[22] This is true, for Scripture says "repent, therefore, and be converted, that your sins may be blotted out ... by the name of Jesus Christ ... for there is no other name under heaven given among men, whereby we must be saved. ... And they said, believe on the Lord Jesus Christ, and thou shalt be saved" (Acts 3:19, 4:10,12, 16:31). We saw that Noah lived by faith and was saved by God's grace. We know that Abraham was to sacrifice his son as a foreshadow of God giving His Son as a sacrifice for our sin. Moses, too, was a type of Christ when he mediated with God for the chosen people of Israel. Until the incarnation of Christ, God tells His people about the coming of the promised Redeemer. Scripture points directly to Him by revealing His part in salvation through the working of His grace in the lives of His chosen people. Now, upon the redemption accomplished by Christ, God's redeeming grace is applied to believers. Consequently, Christians are to cast down reasonings "and every high thing that exalteth itself against the knowledge of God, and bringing into captivity every thought to the obedience of Christ" (II Cor 10:5). Christian educators and parents who affirm the Covenant of Redemption must also affirm the inseparable Covenant of Grace. Yet many Christians only take hold of Redemption and erroneously ignore the fullness of God's grace by failing to actively order the world in all of its aspects and spheres in conformity with the principles of Scripture. In the educational battle for the hearts, souls, and minds of covenant children, "to withhold from pupils the elements of the Christian faith is not only to conceal from them the realities of life but also to deprive them of the only means of meeting the exigencies and cries of life and of fulfilling the great end of their existence. To put it bluntly, it is to damn them to godlessness."[23]

As the life and teachings of Christ are revealed in Scripture by His apostles, the connection of redemption and grace is clear and the significance for education is conclusive. A consistent Christian will order or interpret the world and all of life in such a way that both principles of redemption and of life restoration are brought to their complete and all-pervasive expression and fruition.[24] Christ and His apostles have plainly taught this and the inferences for Christian education are beyond any doubt. Surely, "if the biblical revelation is ultimate for thought, outlook, and practice, we must readily see the implications for education."[25]

* * * * *

Early in Matthew's account of the life of Jesus, we learn that Christ was led by the Spirit of God. It is under the Spirit's direction that Jesus is tempted, and being directed by the Spirit, Jesus says "Begone Satan! For it is written, 'You shall worship the Lord your God, and Him only shalt thou serve'" (Matt 4:10). Throughout the temptation account, the Lord Jesus proclaims the written law of God as His standard for all of life and He does not waiver from this authority.

As Christian parents, educators and students "we have the mind of Christ" (I Cor 2:16). Conversely, non-Christian educators and their schools are not led by the Spirit: "[they] receiveth not the things of the Spirit of God; for they are foolishness unto him, neither can he know them, because they are spiritually discerned" (I Cor 2:14). Clearly, unbelievers do not have the mind of Christ; thus, they cannot teach the mind of Christ to covenant children. Furthermore, unbelieving educators are always in revolt against Jesus' command to worship and serve only the Lord God. They despise and shrink from the law of God as the only authoritative standard. In contrast, "that we might know the things freely given to us by God," (I Cor 2:12) Christian educators say with Jesus, "Begone, Satan!" from all aspects of education, for we shall worship the Lord our God throughout all of education, and Him only shall we serve as we learn and minister for the glory of God. Unbelievers and believers who entrust the education of God's covenant children to secularists miscarry their redemptive obligation to obey Jesus.

* * * * *

"Jesus went about all of Galilee, teaching . . . and preaching the gospel of the Kingdom. . . . And there followed Him great multitudes of people. . . . And when He saw the multitudes . . . He began to teach them" (Matt 4:23,25, 5:1). He said that believers "are the salt of the earth, but if the salt has become tasteless, how will it be made salty again?" (Matt 5:13 N.A.S.B.) Jesus declared that believers "are the light of the world," (Matt 5:14) and that believers should not put their light under a bushel.

Rather, they should determine to let their light shine before men.

In order to be the salt and light of God before men, Jesus explains that He has "not come to destroy the law, or the prophets . . . but to fulfill" (Matt 5:17,18). every jot and tittle. This Christ applies to all believers when He requires that they not "break one of these least commandments" nor shall they teach others to annul God's law, or they "shall be called least in the kingdom of heaven." On the other hand, "whosoever keeps and teaches [all of the Lord's commandments] the same shall be called great in the kingdom of heaven" (Matt 5:19 KJV with N.A.S.B.).

Many Christians desire to be teachers and in so doing rightly fashion themselves after the teaching patterned by Jesus. Some believers want to be the salt and light which Jesus spoke of by evangelizing in the modern public school system, and others by developing Christian schools. Clearly the Master teacher espouses evangelism, but never at the cost of nullifying one jot or one tittle of the Word of God, God's law. Accordingly, Christians who teach in secular schools are missionaries or child-evangelists who present the gospel as opportunities present themselves. They are not teachers who proclaim in all biblical fullness, redemption and grace. There is compromise throughout all their teachings because biblical theism is not the source of state mandated and controlled curriculum. Perverse phantoms of neutrality, utopian aspirations, state decrees and leaders whose authority is Satan in their hearts, have more weight than the Word of God. The Bible is an illegal authority in public schools, while books which attack and denounce Christianity are legal. Clearly, there is bitter hatred of the doctrines of Christ at the core of public education and the presence of the Holy Spirit is vehemently opposed. Jesus "is a stone of stumbling, and a rock of offense . . . being disobedient," (I Pet 2:8); secular educators are not the people of God.

The whole armor of God, which is designed by God for believers to withstand the wiles of the devil, is by law stripped from the saints in state-controlled public schools. It is true that a few indefatigable evangelists find some limited success in these schools; like a plant growing among thorns, it succeeds in forcing a passage through the obstacles of sin, compromise, statism, discouragement, and curriculum which is hostile to Christ, to blossom in the quickening sun of God's grace.

Nonetheless, most Christians that are teaching in these schools must keep the light of Holy Writ under bushels of unrighteousness and withhold the salt of life from seasoning curriculum, administration, teaching methods, extra-curricular activities and students. St. Augustine wrote, "He who for fear of any power hides the truth, provokes the wrath of God to come upon him, for he fears men more than God."[26]

Genuine Christian teaching is like Christ's teaching if redemption and law are taught and kept. Christ's light is to freely shine throughout the entire educational process and not just during evangelism. This can be done in a Christian school that is set on a hill and cannot be hidden. Certainly, evangelism is a part of the Christian teacher's task, but it is not the whole task, for the whole task includes teaching every jot and tittle of the law. In order to complete this task, the salty taste of Christ must be central in the interpretation of every skill and lesson, and it must be actively lived or practiced in service-ministry by both teacher and student. Evangelists proclaim the gospel to lost souls while Christian teachers also instruct believers and their seed to know and abide in the Christian way of life.

* * * * *

Jesus concludes the Sermon on the Mount with a parable. Previously He taught the people the contrast between the Christian way of life and the non-Christian way of life. He ends by illustrating the two different foundations. A Christian way of life is built upon a rock foundation and is able to withstand the rain, floods, and winds because it is based on hearing the sayings of Christ and acting upon them. The non-Christian way of life is built upon the sand and is unable to withstand the rain, floods, and wind because it is not based on hearing and doing the sayings of Christ.

This parable of Jesus is applicable to the sphere of education. Secular educators do not hear or do the sayings of Christ when they build the foundations of public education. The entire secular educational system is built upon the sand of humanism and is unable to stand against the storms. When confronted by the Lord God, the modern public school system will fall. Even if Christian educators do not confront secular schools with the truth, they will fall under their own weight. The sins of godlessness, statism, self-made moral standards, humanistic values, and the deification of man will beat upon the school system and it will fall, and great will be its fall. Consider the problems facing the public schools: daily student drunkenness, 220 assaults reported by teachers in the Cleveland school system, a fifteen-year-old student earning $500 a week selling dope to school children, and the steady decline in S.A.T. scores.[27] Surely, if God were limited to human logic or reason, He would be baffled by the irrationalism of believers who are enamored with building the minds of His children upon the sands, while the Rock, Jesus Christ, our covenant head, stands ready to firmly hold God's school system.

* * * * *

Matthew reports Jesus' teaching about the mysteries of the Kingdom of God by recording parables which Christ set forth to the multitudes. After the parable of the sower, Jesus privately expounded its meaning to the disciples and He revealed why He spoke in parables "because it is given to you to know the mysteries of the kingdom of heaven, but unto them it is not given" (Matt 13:11). In other words, Christ says that the Kingdom of God "remains a secret for the flesh because it runs completely contrary to the expectations of the flesh. ... The flesh does not understand what it means to live by the gift of grace."[28]

Secular educators and their schools, while they remain locked in the flesh of unbelief, do not know the mysteries of the kingdom of heaven, for the Lord Jesus has not given to them the ears for hearing, the eyes for seeing, nor the heart for understanding. They that are after the flesh [unbelieving teachers and students], always frame the thoughts of their mind [teaching and learning] after the things of the flesh. "For the mind [teaching and learning] set on the flesh is hostile toward God; for it does not subject itself to the law of God, for it is not even able to do so; and those who are in the flesh [secular educators] cannot please God" (Rom 8:5-8).

Although Jesus said the mysteries of the Kingdom of God are not given to unbelievers, and thus to secular educators, He also said that these mysteries are given to His disciples, hence to Christian educators. Correspondingly, Christian educators are to be Spirit directed in complete contrast to secular educators who are directed by the flesh. Spirit-directed educators frame the thoughts of their mind (teaching and learning) after the things of the Spirit. For the mind (teaching and learning) set on the Spirit is life and peace. They are in fellowship with the Lord and subject to the law of God, thus Christian educators that are in the Spirit can please God. Some Christian educators believe collaboration is possible between education of the flesh and education of the Spirit. They fail to understand that these two are completely and absolutely exclusive of one another. For the Scripture says, "So then, brethren [Christian educators and students] we are under obligation, not to the flesh [secular schools], to live [actively learn, teach and minister] according to the flesh" but to be led by the Spirit of God, whereby Christian educators and learners "have received the Spirit of adoption and as sons we cry out, Abba! Father!"(Rom 8:12-15).

* * * * *

Jesus said "the kingdom of heaven is like a treasure hidden in a field, which when a man hath found, he hideth, and for the joy of it goeth and selleth all that he hath, and buyeth that field" (Matt 13:44). The kingdom is of such high value to believers that they will give up everything for it. It is so captivating that we do not care to own anything except the kingdom. Then, after revealing these teachings, Christ went to Nazareth where the people were "astonished" at His wisdom and mighty works. But many "took offense at Him," thus "He did not do many works of power there because of their unbelief" (Matt 13:54-58).

Learning God's thoughts after and in the likeness of God, is similar to finding a hidden treasure. Being taught to understand and minister the Word of God by biblically directed Christian educators is a pearl of great price. There should be no wonder why Godly covenant people make considerable sacrifice in order to secure God-conscious education from biblically directed Christian schools. Non-Christian educators and parents are rightly astonished at this revelation of God's grace and take offense. Believing educators and parents who do not seek the grace of God in Christian schools ought not to be surprised that God does not do many works of power in secular schools or in the lives of their children; it is because of unbelief.

* * * * *

In Jerusalem just before His death, Jesus told the parable of the marriage feast. Jesus said the kingdom of heaven is like the king who prepared a great marriage feast for his son and he "sent forth his servants to call them that were bidden to the wedding; and they would not come. . . . But they made light of it, and went their ways . . ." (Matt 22:3,5). So it is with Christian education. The Lord our King has prepared an educational feast for all believers, His adopted sons, and He has called them "that in all things Christ might have the preeminence" (Col 1:18). Yet, many believers grossly insult the King of kings by refusing to support Christian schools. They make light of them and in doing so go their own ways by affiliating with secular educators who are characterized as "them that are defiled and unbelieving, nothing is pure; but even their mind and conscience is defiled" (Titus 1:15).

* * * * *

Jesus was put on trial by Caiaphus and the Sanhedrin. His testimony was elicited in order to condemn Him and then to reject Him. Accordingly, Jesus was sentenced to death for "He hath spoken blasphemy!" (Matt 26:65). The children of Israel, the seed of Abraham, rejected their promised Redeemer. God's anointed covenant head, by whom His redemptive grace is given, was rebuffed and "they spat in His face" (Matt 26:67). Judas betrayed Him and Peter denied his Lord.

Unbelieving educators also put Christ on trial in order to condemn Him and then to reject His authority over all of education. They sentence to educational death Jesus and all those who believe that Christ is relevant to contemporary education, because to affirm Jesus as God is to blaspheme the sovereignty of man. Furthermore, believing educators and parents who confederate with secular educators claim to educate on common ground. Very subtly this false belief infiltrates the minds of covenant children. They begin to think that a vast volume of secular facts exist rather than comprehending all facts in their relationship to God. For example, someone might say "George Washington was the first president of the United States" and believe that this is a common ground fact - a neutral fact that may be equally comprehended by both Christians and non-Christians. This educational craftsmanship cannot remain unchallenged. The fact that Washington was the first president must be comprehended in a context: God's context or man's context. Consequently common ground, if it existed, would exclude Christ and be "on par with Judas' act of betrayal."[29] In contrast, Christian schools which are founded on God's covenant, exist to exemplify Christ throughout the entire educational system, particularly as essential for understanding every fact.

* * * * *

On the Sabbath after the death of Christ, his mother went to His tomb. It was early morning when there appeared an angel of the Lord. The angel answered Mary Magdalene and the other Mary, "Fear not; for I know that ye seek Jesus, who was crucified. He is not here; for He is risen, ... He is risen from the dead" (Matt 28:5-7). On the way to Galilee, "Jesus met them saying, 'All hail.' And they came and held Him by the feet, and worshipped Him. Then Jesus said unto them, 'Be not afraid; go tell My brethren that they go into Galilee, and there they shall see Me'" (Matt 28:9,10). At the same time that Jesus revealed Himself, the guards informed "the chief priests all the things that were done" (Matt 23:11). Immediately their reaction was disbelief. Further, they conspired with the elders to deny Christ's resurrection, Christ's power, and Christ's authority in heaven and on earth.

These two powers still contest each other in all of the world and particularly in education. Today's unbelieving educators place all of their educational practice in the service of the lie fostered by the chief priests. In absolute contrast to Christ's words, "All hail" and the worship given Him by the brethren, non-Christian educators deny the resurrection of Christ and they refuse to acclaim the Lord's power and authority in every aspect of education. Accordingly, a coalition between these two powers is impossible unless compromise is present on the part of the believing educators or parents. A temporary alliance for the education of covenant children in secular schools or by unbelieving educators is accommodating the lie first developed by the chief priests and is robbing Christ of all His rightful acclaim and worship. Unbelieving educators or an alliance with them will not nurture covenant students to be prepared to "Go .. . and teach all nations ... teaching them to observe all things whatsoever I have commanded you ..." (Matt 28:19,20) because the commandments of Christ are denied by all unbelieving educators or by the terms of any educational alliance they enter. "Don't you know that friendship with the world is hatred toward God?" (James 4:4).

* * * * *

Many further accounts from Jesus' life, His teaching, and from the apostles are given in Scripture. They clearly illustrate God's covenant of redemption and man's educational responsibility. Certainly it is clear that Jesus came to liberate "all that the Father hath given" (John 6:37) from Satan, and that conflict with Satan is inevitable and irreconcilable apart from Christ. The demons call Jesus the "Holy One of God" (Mk 1:24). They recognize His authority "and they do obey Him" (Mk 1:27). Although unbelieving educators are not demon-possessed as some of the people in Capernaum were, in a different way, they are in Satan's power. They walk in darkness. They teach and learn in darkness. Secular education does not recognize that Jesus is the light of the world. Some believing educators and parents fail to recognize this and to obey Him when Jesus says, "he that followeth Me shall not walk in darkness," (John 3:12) because they have allied with darkness to educate their children. Allegiance to the promised Redeemer is compromised, devotion to the covenant Head is surrendered, and "the light of life" is dimmed when Christian parents educate the children of God in public schools. Secularists are aliens from the commonwealth of the kingdom of God "and strangers from the covenants of promise, having no hope, and without God," (Eph 2:12) in their educational system. But now, in covenant with Christ Jesus, we "who once were far off are made near by the blood of Christ." This closeness is enhanced by God's school system which is built upon the foundation of the prophets and apostles. Jesus Christ, Himself being the chief cornerstone, is the full-blooded revolutionary who calls for a total world revolution.

Summary

Biblical Christian schools are built four-square on the Lord God of Scripture and His covenant foundations for His people, and only out of building blocks quarried there. Any other foundation or building block is created in or quarried from the minds of men who are in rebellion from the covenant God, the Redeemer. Cooperation for building Christian minds is not possible without compromise of the basic tenets of God's Word, for "the man without the Spirit [the unbelieving educator] does not accept the things that come from the Spirit of God, for they are foolishness to him, and he cannot comprehend them, because they are spiritually discerned" (I Cor 2:14). Therefore, schools which are constructed by man apart from God's covenant are without the Spirit of God and are in opposition to the Lord and to schools which are directed by God's covenanting Spirit.

Early in history God said to Abraham, "Thou shalt keep my covenant therefore, thou, and thy seed after thee in their generation" (Gen 17:9). Accordingly, God said "For I know Abraham, that he will command his children and his household after him, and they shall keep the way of the Lord, to do righteousness and justice. . . ." (Gen 18:19). Abraham kept his covenant responsibility to the Lord by educating his progeny in the way of the Lord. This is part of his faithful response to God in grateful acknowledgement of having received covenantal blessings. Such a Spirit-motivated response is the only kind of response which is acceptable for Abraham and for Christians today because "they who are of the faith, the same are the sons of Abraham" (Gal 3:7).

Although the covenant with Abraham, Isaac and Jacob was individual, it was also a community covenant. The Israelites were joined together as a covenant nation. Today too, Christians are to be joined together as the church, a covenant community of believers, the Israel of the Twentieth Century. Today, Christian believers, who are the sons of Abraham, are to join together without compromising the Word of God in order to conduct their covenantal community obligations. To educate children in the way of the Lord, according to the commandments and statutes of the law, and to love mercy, to do justice, to walk humbly with God are indisputable covenant obligations which every believer must always seriously exercise.[30]

NOTES

1. John Murray COLLECTED WRITINGS OF JOHN MURRAY Vol. 4 (Carlisle, PA: The Banner of Truth Trust, 1982), p.216.

2. O. Palmer Robertson THE CHRIST OF THE COVENANTS (Phillipsburg, NJ: Presbyterian and Reformed Publishing Company, 1980), p.4.

3. *Ibid.,* p.25.

4. *Ibid.,* p.204.

5. S. G. De Graaf PROMISE AND DELIVERANCE Vol.1 Trans., H. and E. Runner (Presbyterian and Reformed Publishing Company, 1979), p.25.

6. Note: The covenant during the Adamic Administration is commonly called the Covenant of Works. The author prefers the designation Covenant of Life which is used by both the Larger and Shorter Westminster Catechisms. See John Murray COLLECTED WRITINGS OF JOHN MURRAY Vol.4, pp. 217-222.

7. S. G. De Graaf PROMISE AND DELIVERANCE Vol.1, p.29.

8. Cornelius Van Til ESSAYS ON CHRISTIAN EDUCATION (Presbyterian and Reformed Publishing Company, 1974), p.124.

9. John Murray COLLECTED WRITINGS OF JOHN MURRAY Vol.4, p.229.

10. Samuel L. Blumenfeld IS PUBLIC EDUCATION NECESSARY? (Boise, ID: The Paradigm Co., 1985), p.2.

11. Cornelius Van Til A CHRISTIAN THEORY OF KNOWLEDGE (Presbyterian and Reformed Publishing Company, 1969), p.259.

12. S. G. De Graaf PROMISE AND DELIVERANCE Vol.II, p.11.

13. *Ibid.,* p.22

14. Walter Karp *Why Johnny Can't Think* THE PLAIN DEALER, May 19, 1985, p.1-B. Note: This quote is taken from *A Place Called School* written by John Goodlad after an eight year study of thirty-eight public schools.

15. H. Richard Niebuhr CHRIST AND CULTURE (NY: Harper Colophon Books, 1951), p.1.

16. *Ibid.,* p.9.

17. S. G. De Graaf PROMISE AND DELIVERANCE Vol.2, p.348.

18. *Ibid.*, p.431.

19. H. Richard Niebuhr CHRIST AND CULTURE p.23.

20. Eugen Rosenstock-Hussy OUT OF REVOLUTION: AUTOBIOGRAPHY OF WESTERN MAN (Norwich, VT: Argo Books, 1969), p.217.

21. John Murray COLLECTED WRITINGS OF JOHN MURRAY Vol.4, p.238.

22. A FAITH TO CONFESS: THE BAPTIST CONFESSION OF FAITH OF 1689, rewritten in modern English (Sussex, England: Carey Publications, 1975), p.27.

23. John Murray COLLECTED WRITINGS OF JOHN MURRAY Vol.4, p.371.

24. *Ibid.*, p.357.

25. *Ibid.*, p.368.

26. J. H. Mark d'Auligne THE REFORMATION IN ENGLAND Vol.2 (Carlisle, PA: The Banner of Truth Trust, 1985) p.41.

27. Edward P. Whalen *I Will Not Push, Kick, Stab or Shoot the Teacher,* CLEVELAND MAGAZINE, September, 1977, pp.64-65; *Academic Slump Hits Whiz Kidz, Too* U.S. NEWS AND WORLD REPORT, March 16, 1981, p. 12; Steven Miller, *Universities are Turning Out Highly Skilled Barbarians* U.S. NEWS AND WORLD REPORT, November 10, 1980, pp.57-58; *A Sink-or-Swim Approach to Education* THE PLAIN DEALER, August 20, 1986, p.13A.

28. S. G. De Graaf PROMISE AND DELIVERANCE Vol.3, p.80.

29. *Ibid.*, Vol.4, p.153.

30. Joel Belz *Too Little Money for What You Believe In* PRESBYTERIAN JOURNAL, June 5, 1985, pp.6-8. Note: Belz presents the educational implications for covenant community obligations having significant impact upon Christian school finance. Grace Christian School, in Cleveland, Ohio, has used the covenant community obligation approach to finances since its inception.

PART II
The Biblical Foundation - Basic Considerations

Before Christian education can be put into action, there are several basic considerations which must be investigated. Many well intentioned Christian leaders and parents begin Christian schools or become involved with established Christian schools without first examining the nature of Christian education. This is like shooting an arrow in the air and then looking to find the target. The key elements need to be discussed prior to jumping into the educational process. Sometimes this step is called giving attention to the idea of constructing a Christian philosophy of education or to those in academia, "epistemological self-consciousness."

1. Christian Presuppositions

Biblical Christian schools are ultimately started by educators who listen "with loving obedience to God Who identifies Himself to man in Christ as his creator and redeemer. . . . [Christian educators, parents, and students] accept the Word for what it is by the inward work of the Holy Spirit, bearing witness by and with the Word in their hearts."[1] Christian schools are begun with the belief that "what the Bible says about God and His revelation to the universe as unquestionably true on its own authority."[2]

Within the above are suppositions which underlie and direct all that Christians do. These suppositions are called biblical presuppositions which alone should govern all that is done in Christian education. However, these presuppositions "have never been located and systematically set forth for Christian educators to consider."[3] In fact, many pagan presuppositions have been integrated into Christian schools by Christian educators because they have failed to identify Christian presuppositions and to contrast them with non-Christian presuppositions. Accordingly, an introductory survey of the biblical presuppositions is presented.

First, God exists. The sovereign triune God of Christianity exists and "faith in God precedes understanding everything else."[4]

Second, the Bible is the Word of God revealed to the prophets and apostles and written by them without error.

Third, God reveals himself in Christ "through Scripture understood properly by the regeneration of the Holy Spirit."[5]

The above presuppositions establish the starting points for Christian schools and Christian education which are founded upon the covenant God has made with man. They stand in complete opposition to or in antithesis with the presuppositions of non-Christians. It is impossible for a person to hold to these beliefs and also hold to the opposite of these beliefs. For example, a person cannot believe that God exists and then in faith interpret the universe while simultaneously believing that God does not exist and is unnecessary for genuine learning. A school system cannot believe in faith that the Bible is the inerrant Word of God and also doubt that the Bible is the Word of God. Educators cannot esteem that a special regenerating act of the Holy Spirit is indispensable for Christian faith and living and believe too that the regeneration of the Holy Spirit is unnecessary for learning or teaching.

In complete contrast to the above three presuppositions are the following non-Christian presuppositions.

First, man exists as the final reference point for what is affirmed or denied, true or false, and right or wrong.

Second, the universe has evolved into existence and facts (for example, the law of gravity) were always "just there" by chance.

Third, the laws of logic and reason are accepted as legislative for what man can or cannot accept as possible or probable.[6]

In brief, "the essence of the non-Christian position is that man is assumed to be ultimate or autonomous."[7] This presupposition is the heart of secular humanism and is found as the root of all secularist thought and action. With this assumption the non-Christian virtually places himself in the position that God holds in Christianity and, thus, stands in absolute conflict with biblical presuppositions. For example, a person cannot believe both sovereign man and sovereign God are the final reference point for what is affirmed or denied. A school system cannot teach that the universe has evolved into existence by chance plus millions of years, and also teach that biblical creation is true. Educators cannot claim that the laws of logic or reason are legislative for learning, education, truth and living while professing that the Bible is man's absolute and final authority for all matters.

Educators that promote Christian education and Christian schools need to be knowledgeable about the contrast between the Christian presuppositions and non-Christian presuppositions. These Christian leaders must be certain that in understanding and in practice students are always conscious of these distinctions. It is not enough for Christian school students to be tested on the content of these facts and get an "A" or "100%" correct. Christian school students who have learned the distinction must live a Christian way of life which continuously demonstrates the convictions of a Christian mind. Nothing short of this is the goal of Christian education.

The three key Christian presuppositions are the starting points for Christian schools and Christian education. They must be well understood. In addition, other essential biblical presuppositions which are derived from them must be identified and their relevancy to Christian education explored.

* * * * *

First, the existence of God is not to be taken lightly in Christian education. God cannot be esteemed as a matter of fact, which Christian students believe, and be irrelevant to learning and life. Nor can the Lord God be reduced to being an "additive" or "integrative" factor which supposedly Christianizes education. Christian students are to comprehend the Lord with a continuous, all-encompassing, God-conscious mind. The Lord is never to be absent from directing a Christian student's way of thinking or living. Christian teachers, like Christian parents, are to be used by the Spirit of God to guide their children in understanding God's unceasing regulation over all thoughts, things, and actions - over all of education.

Faith in the sovereign triune God of Scripture is a prerequisite to learning God's thoughts after God. A student who does not submit in faith to the Lord God stands in rebellion from God and cannot comprehend God's way for Christians to learn and minister. God, through the power of His Spirit, enables students, by faith in God, to be free of sin and to receive "the mind of Christ" (I Cor 2:16). It is after the Spirit gives faith in God to the learner that the learner may then "know the things that are freely given to us of God" (I Cor 2:12) or develop a robust God-consciousness for Christian living.

* * * * *

Second, the sovereign God of the universe speaks with absolute authority. "It is Christ as God who speaks in the Bible. Therefore, the Bible does not appeal to human reason as ultimate in order to justify what it says. It comes to the human being with absolute authority."[8] Accordingly, the Bible is necessary for all learning; it is always relevant; and it is the standard for all educational practice. The whole Bible is to be unbroken in its union with the mind and life of Christian students. There is no alternative for Christian educators, Christian parents, or Christian students if their Christian distinction is to be maintained without compromise.

The Bible is the written Word of God and as such has certain attributes which carry educational significance. These attributes are the Bible's necessity, authority, clarity and sufficiency. They are important suppositions about the Bible and are biblical presuppositions which regulate its usage.

The Bible is necessary "supernatural word communication" from God and is the means God has used, through the Spirit, "to tell man of his destiny and to make him" aware of God's covenant.[9] Without this revelation from God all men, including their educational systems, are lost in sin, confused and directionless. The Bible is necessary if students are to know where they came from, to know their standing before God, and to know their purpose in life.

Biblical authority is vital for Christian educators. Without this authority educators must establish for themselves their own authority; they must create their own values or moral code, and allow their students the freedom to "clarify" or develop their own standards for life. In sharp contrast, Christian educators believe that "whatever is in accord with Scripture is educative; whatever is not in accord with it is miseducative. Difficult as it may be for both the teacher and the pupil to make out in individual instances how to apply this criterion, the criterion itself is plain and simple enough."[10]

The authority of the Bible was a keystone of the Reformation. Either the authority of the Church and popery or that of Scripture was supreme. The reformers went straight to the torch of heaven, the fountain of truth, which is the very Word of God. On the other hand, the Roman clergy placed the Church above Scripture. The laws of Rome were above the Word of God. Without the Bible as their authority, the people were in an age of spiritual slavery.

On September 23, 1413, Sir John Cobham, an Englishman who followed the teachings of Wycliffe,

> ... was taken before the ecclesiastical tribunal then sitting at St. Paul's. "We must believe," said the primate to him, "what the holy church of Rome teaches, without demanding Christ's authority." "Believe!" shouted the priests, "Believe!" - "I am willing to believe all that God desires," said Sir John, "but that the pope should have authority to teach what is contrary to Scripture - that I can never believe!" ... Then holding the sentence of death in his hand, [Arundel, a priest] read it with a loud clear voice. ... [Later, Sir John was] dragged on a hurdle to St. Gile's fields, and there suspended by chains over a slow fire, and cruelly burned to death.[11]

Clearly, public schools run by the state are no different than the pre-reformation Church of Rome under papal authority. The authority of the Bible is usurped by state authority. The laws of the state are above the Word of God. The people who are enamored by these state schools are in spiritual slavery because the authority of Scripture - our Truth which will set us free - is suppressed by secular and state tribunals. The state-approved curriculum is the Bibleless authority in the classroom. Through it students are led to believe in statism, socialism, situational ethics, the deity of democracy and a host of unscriptural heresies. These schools hold the sentence of death in their teaching, curriculum and philosophy. To be sure, many of God's children have been suspended by the chains of secular humanism, placed over the slow fire of Bibleless curriculum and cruelly burned to death by the teaching of unbelievers.

The Bible is "plain and simple enough" to understand because God has clearly revealed Himself to man. Students and educators, under the direction of the Holy Spirit, require no human interpreter to comprehend what God says in His Word. Teachers may guide them, but Spirit-guided students, with reading ability, can understand the biblical message and apply its meaning to their education and thus to their lives.

Sufficiency of the Bible means that the Scriptures need no additions or subtractions. In the Bible, God has given to His people all that they need to know. Christian educators and students ought not to be looking for additional supernatural revelation from the Lord nor should they be ignoring any part of the Bible. The Spirit of God uses the written Word of God to reveal God's will to His people in a manner that is sufficient for the Christian way of life.

* * * * *

The third key presupposition for Christian education is the belief that Jesus Christ is who He claimed to be - the Son of God, Immanuel. Jesus is the Redeemer, the promised Messiah. His righteousness is ascribed or imputed to His people by the special regenerating action of the Holy Spirit. This work of God in the lives of His people is indispensable for education to be Christian. "Biblically speaking, it is fair to say that Christian education truly begins for a student only when he is saved: 'the fear of the Lord is the *beginning* of wisdom.'"[12] The Holy Spirit seals the Covenant of Redemption with each new Christian by indwelling him and enabling him to "take captive every thought to make it obedient to Christ" (II Cor 10:5). Subsequently, in grateful acknowledgement of God's grace, believers seek to execute their covenant obligations by faithfully starting and supporting Christ-honoring Christian schools. They want to serve Christ by serving and ministering to all people at all times. This includes education, particularly in each and every learning activity.

Derived from the above three presuppositions are several other essential biblical teachings which are vital for education to be Christian. Christian educators and students cannot overlook these teachings. They, too, must always govern the union of factual content and skills with teaching and ministering.

These biblical teachings will be called "presuppositions" because for Christians these teachings are biblical truths which must fence in and guide, with authoritative direction, all the thoughts and activities of believers. They are up-front biblical faith principles which are always to frame the minds of Christians. They have been accepted as indispensable biblical truths. Without them Christianity and Christian education fails.

Creation Presuppositions

The Bible teaches that "God created the heavens and the earth" (Gen 1:1). This belief is a biblical presupposition which must rule the minds of Christian students. The creationist believes and teaches the fact that God is eternal and timeless while everything else was made in time by God. This teaching is to continuously direct the Christian educator and learner.

Adding the creation perspective to the curriculum or to a specific lesson is impotent. Attempts to integrate creationism into the teaching-learning process are also untenable. If the truth of creationism is not present in the minds of Christian educators and learners at the outset of the teaching-learning process then the truth of creationism is reduced to being probably true or possibly correct. The criterion or standard for understanding is no longer the Bible. Rather, man becomes the standard for truth because it is up to him, or in this case, the teacher or student to bring creationism to influence learning. It is ludicrous for Christian teachers to attempt to add or integrate the creation beliefs into a student's mind or to attach it to factual content because the Christian educator and student already presuppose and actively know that their minds and all things were created by God.

Is it not true that one of the first things taught children or new Christians is that it was "God, who made the world and all things in it ... seeing He giveth to all life and breath, and all things"? (Acts 17:24,25). Once the Holy Spirit gives the faith necessary for this understanding then the creation presupposition permanently regulates all other thoughts and actions, all subsequent learning. Clearly additive or integrative teaching or learning processes are inconceivable nonsense because after the Holy Spirit has implanted this teaching in the hearts of believers, it becomes the Christians' way of thinking. It is unimaginable for believers, including children, to substitute the evolutionist view of origins for their creationist belief. Nor is it biblically correct to assume that the student's mind is an empty void or blank slate waiting for creationist concepts to be added or integrated into it.

Believing educators and students think and live with the creationist belief shaping all of their learning. It is not true that believing students look at a tree and then try to add on or integrate into their creationist beliefs the facts they observe from the tree. Believing students know that the tree is created prior to their observation. Teachers need not add or integrate the creationist belief into the students perspective of the tree. Teachers are to guide, direct, shape, instruct and draw out the Christian student's creationist belief and aid the student in applying it to whatever is being considered. Creationist belief is then further developed by the student, under the teacher's supervision through the discovery of "new" creation facts and the glorification of God by actually using the facts for ministry or service to the Lord.

When this latter teaching approach is used, students will always be learning within the bounds of biblical Christian education. Teachers do not need to ask, "How do we add creation to science?" or "How do we integrate a psychological concept with a biblical concept?" because the two concepts are and have always been *integrally* related. In contrast, Christian teachers should ask, "How can we enhance or facilitate in the students' learning experiences the relationship that has always existed between the created facts and God, the sovereign and almighty One?" The answer to this legitimate question is to develop an educational system which is built completely and only upon biblical presuppositions.

The Bible and the creation presuppositions have been briefly presented. However, for Christian learning to take place, the relationship between the Bible and creation revelation must also be understood by Christian educators and students. The relationship is that the Bible and creation revelation are supplementary and reciprocal. In other words, the two forms of God's self-revelation are interdependent. The Bible needs the creation revelation in order to have something to represent the written words, and creation revelation needs God's biblical words in order to explain its relationship to Him, its Creator. It is the power of the Holy Spirit which makes this complementary relationship actualize in the minds of Christian learners. However, Christians must always keep in mind that this is an unequal reciprocal relationship because the creation revelation is under the curse of sin while the Bible is God's Word, and thus, in its original form, is above sin. The result of understanding this important relationship is that Christian educators need not be confused by thinking that there are two sources of truth or that it appears to be multifaceted. God's revelation is a three-in-one unity: the Bible, creation revelation, and the power of the Holy Spirit. If this unity is broken, Christian learning is aborted.

2. Man Created in the Image of God

The belief that God created man in His image is a biblical presupposition which ought never to be forgotten. This teaching is common in most Christian schools but its educational influence has been seriously restricted. Since being created in the image of God means that God made each person like God in every way that a creature can be like God, this biblical teaching is broad in scope. It includes the concepts that man is religious, moral, rational and individualistic. Furthermore, man was created with an innate "dominion" purpose which is to result in ministry for the glory of God. Each of these biblical attributes of man underlie the Christian educator's view of himself and of every student. In addition, these concepts should always be pressed upon the process of Christian education with the realization that man is finite and limited to time while God is infinite, timeless and unchangeable.

(a) Man was created as a religious being; to worship the Lord like no other created creature or thing. Worship of the Lord is to be a constant activity throughout every aspect of human life. Education is no exception. Christian educators and students will exhibit their faith with reverence, devotion, and adoration for their Creator God. Praise and acknowledgement of the Lord will steadily stream out of biblical Christian schools because the believers there are taught to be God-conscious in all their ways. This stands in complete contrast to the non-Christian religious faith with its humanistic religious character that worships the genius, man or some other aspect of creation.

Non-Christian educators, in secular fashion, attempt to be non-religious or non-spiritual in their educational practices. They want people to believe that they leave spiritual instruction to the auspices of the home and church. In reality, this "antagonism of modern, tolerant culture to Christ is of course often disguised because it does not call its religious practices religious, reserving that term for certain specified rites connected with officially recognized sacred institutions."[13] This is true. Secular or statist public schools are sacred institutions which practice religious rites in all of their educational practices because they are patterned after the worship of man as god of the universe. The question is not whether or not religious or spiritual education is to be included as part of the educational system. Rather, the question is, "Which religion will govern education: biblical religion or some other type?" All of life is religious so there is no escape from the spiritual dimension.

(b) All men are moral creations. Man was created to live in a righteous and holy relationship with God his Maker. This means that at no time is man not actively thinking or acting in a truly righteous and holy relationship with the Lord God or in an unrighteous and unholy relationship with God. Consequently, all the events taking place in the classroom are morally right before God or they are immoral before Him. All of education, including the entire teaching-learning process, like all of life, has moral standing before God. Education and life itself are not amoral or neutral in any way.

The moral dimension of man has major significance for Christian educators in contrast to secular educators. Since secular educators never are in a righteous and holy relationship with the Lord they never teach or shape students in a morally righteous or holy manner. They can only lead students away from a morally right relationship with the Lord. Christian parents who enroll their children in secular schools subject God's covenant children to a continuous bombardment of immoral teaching, experiences, role models, lessons, and other related activities. In fact, many times they are actively encouraged or required to neglect their Christian convictions while at school. Thus, they are inspired to sin by the teaching-learning process of secularists.

Christian educators, too, must beware of being caught up in immoral teaching patterns. Jay Adams affirms this when he writes, "Christian educators are unaware of the fact that, in almost every essential, Christian education as it is currently practiced is based on humanistic presuppositions, works towards humanistic goals, and follows humanistic practices."[14] For example, humanism is rampant in Christian school curriculum selection, classroom rules, grading systems, testing procedures, teacher evaluation, and goals or objectives set for student development. Certainly when humanistic activities take place in Christian schools, immoral practices are happening. Immoral humanistic activities must be expelled, root and branch, from Christian education and from Christian schools. Christian schools need to be rebuilt from the covenant foundation upwards, and to stop fashioning themselves after the secular pattern exemplified by modern public schools. The case ought to be reversed. Secular and statist public schools should be fashioning themselves after the pattern of Christian schools because the latter are rightly established according to the Word of God.

Christian educators who teach and administer in secular schools and parents who enroll God's covenant children in them will find it difficult, if not impossible, to be free of the humanist immoral influence. Since all that unbelievers ever think or do, and consequently teach, is in an immoral context, then immorality is continuously being presented before Christians in secular schools. Extreme pressure is put on Christian teachers to copulate with humanistic thinking and practices. This is clearly evident in the requirement to instruct from secular curriculum guides, textbooks, workbooks, and with recommended teaching methodologies where the humanistic view is authoritative and the biblical view is virtually nonexistent or reduced to absurd nonsense. This immoral context is readily evident in the non-Christian view of the learner. They view learners as basically good and free of the myth of sin. Such a view is false and immoral because it is clearly in violation of biblical teaching (Rom 3:10-12).

Furthermore, covenant students in secular schools are required to produce secular answers for "good grades." Straight A's can be earned by any student in secular schools without ever mentioning God or making reference to the Bible. Christian students in these schools begin to believe that success can be had while biblical truth is nullified. We believe that they are, therefore, constantly being shaped by the immoral humanistic mold of the secular classroom. They are never presented the truth of Christ as the Truth which is always present in all factual content. Thus, an immoral way of thinking and living replaces or confronts the biblical view taught at home and in church. This confrontation of immoral secular teaching is easily identified by Christian educators and students when major issues such as creation versus evolution or the reality of Christ as opposed to the mythical view, are before them. Perhaps most covenant students will stand firm on these issues. However they do not have the ability to comprehend and withstand the confrontation over every issue, fact or teaching. Indeed secular educators would never tolerate the continuous confrontation of Christ in their classrooms. Furthermore, the Christian teacher in the secular school is not free to deviate from the secular curriculum in order to entertain every claim of Christ. "No fact can be known unless it be known in its relationship to God."[15] If this relationship is ever aborted then immorality is present because God is blasphemed.

Morality is a primary concern of the National Association of Christian Educators (N.A.C.E.). This is an organization of Christian teachers and parents who work in public schools. Their "ultimate goal ... is to reach America's 50,000,000 students with training in academic skills and the life-changing moral and spiritual values they need to live a rewarding, successful life."[16] They, too, desire biblical moral standards and want to implant them in public schools. This is nice for our country and evangelizing our nations youth in accord with the Bible. To be sure, the N.A.C.E.'s work in combating humanism, the National Education Association, teenage pregnancy, homosexual teachers, and obscene textbooks will benefit our country. However, this is not enough. It falls far short of a full-orbed biblical Christian education. Christ and the Bible must be upheld as the sure foundation for all morals, without compromise or accommodation. Accordingly, our efforts as Christian educators must include a distinctly biblical view of knowledge (epistemology), creation (metaphysics), the teaching-learning process (pedagogy), the nature of the learner (anthropology), and morals (axiology). In short, a radically new educational system is needed for Christian students and the answer is God's school system of uncompromisingly biblical Christian schools. Machen's words are to the point. He says:

> Indeed, religion and ethics in Him [Jesus] were never separated; no single element in His life can be understood without reference to His heavenly Father. Jesus was the most religious man who ever lived; He did nothing and said nothing and thought nothing without the thought of God. If His example means anything at all, it means that a human life without the conscious presence of God - even though it

be a life of humanitarian service outwardly like the ministry of Jesus - is a monstrous perversion.[17]

(c) Man, because he is made in the image of God, is a rational being. Man is able to think, to think intelligently, to offer an explanation, and to be reasonable. Often it means to have common sense. A student's ability to think or to be reasonable is assumed by all educators. But, it is the Christian educator who "cannot subject the authoritative pronouncements of Scripture about reality to the scrutiny of reason because it is reason itself that learns its proper function from Scripture."[18] Christian educators and learners stand at opposite poles from non-Christians because they submit the ability to be reasonable or logical to the authority of the Bible while non-Christians believe this ability is neutral and is to be used to determine what is possible and impossible. Logical thinking or reasoning is a created gift from God. It was given to Christian educators that they might teach students to order God's creation revelation.

Some Christian educators fail to clearly submit reason wholly to Scripture. Christians need to watch for this error. Take, for example, what Frank E. Gaebelein writes when he attempts to "determine the truth." He says, "There are three approaches to this matter: from the point of view of revelation alone, from the point of view of revelation plus reason, and from the point of view of reason only. We have already gone far enough to have made a choice: ours is the approach by way of revelation plus reason."[19] Another illustration is provided by A.A. Baker, vice-president of A Beka Book Publications. Baker, in his promotion of *Traditional Christian Education* repeatedly equates the biblical authority with "common sense," and "philosophical thinking grounded in common sense."[20]

In the above examples, the educators fail to clearly subordinate man's reason or his logical explanations to Scripture. Reason and common sense appear to be upheld as being on the same level as the Bible. To be sure, reason and common sense are revelational of God but because of sin are never to be considered as co-equal with Scripture. When a student or teacher is attempting to determine the truth, the entire reasoning process must yield to biblical authority if the education is to be Christian. If all truth is God's truth then God's self-revelation alone is sufficient to determine the truth. God alone is exhaustively rational and from this position God reveals the only all-sufficient foundation for logical reason and common sense, the Bible. Therefore, reason and common sense need not be promoted by Christian educators as being independent from God because the basis of this independence is the humanistic position of human autonomy. It is a messianic humanity which worships the majesty of man.

The above problems with reason and common sense are not limited to educational theory; they affect classroom curriculum. Christian educators and students who rely on "revelation plus reason" or "common sense and the Bible" will not learn that God alone is the final reference point for determining the truth. Rather, they will be led to believe that reason or common sense and God's revelation meet originally in the mind of man, not God.[21] In other words, while both Gaebelein and Baker deny the radical separation between the secular and sacred realms, their existence is still presupposed.[22] Christian school students and teachers become inescapably confused for they can never reconcile the two. The "principle of integration - a deliberate synthesis within the curriculum of the sacred and secular"[23] is supposed to solve the problem. Actually, this reduces a Christian school to be identical to a Roman Catholic school except the theology is protestant and Christian educators attempt to reconcile reason and God's revelation while Catholic educators separate nature and grace. In these Christian schools, both Christian teachers and students are trying to create a Christian perspective (a Kantian notion) which is actually a denial that God alone is the Creator. All the curriculum content or facts were created by God, thus, it is God who also provided the Christian perspective or the actual meaning ascribed to any and every part of the universe. "Reason and revelation should not be contrasted as two sources of knowledge"[24] by Christian educators. Curriculum content, facts, and reason were all created by God and cannot be known apart from God's biblical revelation. For the classroom to be a Christian classroom, reason and common sense must always be subjected to Scripture.

(d) *People are individually and uniquely created in the image of God.* They differ in personality traits, physical abilities, and thinking abilities; yet, they are all equally created in the image of God. Christian educators know that students have different likes and dislikes, have diversified speeds of development, need a variety of learning experiences for understanding, are given multiform gifts and talents, and are involved in all manners of ministry. In brief, students are not all the same in their characteristics but are equivalently created in the image of God.

This individual aspect of each student must be a presupposition which directs the educational process. To be sure, in the area of evangelism, Christians assert that each person must individually stand before God and must individually have a "personal relationship with Jesus Christ." Numerous evangelistic methods, procedures, steps, tactics and practices are conducted in order to evangelize the world. Not all of them are good but they do assume the biblical teaching that all people are different individual personalities. Similarly, Christian educators must individualize the teaching-learning process. Every covenant learner is custom-made by God and is under the shaping power of the Holy Spirit. The Spirit directs them by the Word of God to be custom-formed in the likeness of Christ as ministers for Christ through the teaching of Christian leaders.

Furthermore, God created man as the crown of His creation. Man was placed over all of God's creation, for He declared, "and let them have dominion over the fish of the sea, and over the fowl of the air, and over the cattle, and over all the earth, and over every creeping thing that creepeth upon the earth" (Gen 1:26). Therefore, man is to have authority over creation and no aspect of creation is to rule over him. God gave to man the task of developing Godly culture. Man is to subdue the earth and its creatures for the glory of God. Yet, in our systems of Christian education, it is the curriculum that has dominion over students and it is the curriculum that has the authority to subdue them. Biblically, students should have the dominion and the authority to subdue curriculum. With full consciousness of biblical authority and law, their individual needs, talents, gifts, and interests must have clear priority over curriculum. Curriculum is not to rule in the classroom. Teachers, working with students and their parents, are to rule over curriculum. Each student is to carry out this task before God. In order for us to assist students to fulfill God's mandate, school curriculum must be tailor-made for each student to biblically rule over in their teaching-learning process for the ministry and glory of God. Consequently, the traditional curriculum found in most Christian and secular schools is contrary to biblical principles and must be completely reorganized.

On the whole most Christian schools fail to take this uniqueness aspect beyond evangelism and they rarely apply these individual principles to curriculum content. They tend to hold them in reserve as extracurricular. Notably, the Accelerated Christian Education program (A.C.E.) does take into account variable student learning rates with their booklets or PACE materials. Each student progresses at his or her own rate to complete the pace, to be tested over the curriculum content, and to advance to the next booklet. Individual help is also a positive part of the A.C.E. program. Unfortunately, the A.C.E. program does not go far enough. The grading system, the pre-packaged curriculum content, the teaching methods, the learning activities or projects, and the ministry development for each student enrolled in an A.C.E. program are not individualized. In fact, due to its regimentation, some say that A.C.E. is almost a cult.

Traditional Christian education is the chief offender against biblical principles of student individuality. A Beka Book Publications produces a traditional type of curriculum. It is not unusual to find a traditional school classroom filled with twenty-five fourth grade students reading the same history book at the same rate, and working on the same questions from the same page numbers. Nor is it uncommon to find these same students all working from the same spelling workbook, learning the same list of words, and doing the same spelling exercises. The traditional educator teaching history from his grade-level textbook makes no adjustment for the student's reading level variance which could easily range from the low second grade level to a high tenth grade level. In a spelling lesson, some students may already know all the words on the new spelling list while others may need to learn half or all of the words. Before their spelling workbook is given to them at the beginning of the school year, it is not rare or odd to find some elementary school students in every class who can spell eighty or ninety percent of the spelling words contained in the workbook.

I once had a fourth grade student who boasted that she misspelled only five words in her entire third grade year. She had been using the A Beka spelling curriculum, which was not adjusted to compensate for her ability to spell at the eighth grade level. When her spelling curriculum was personalized to include lists of words that challenged her spelling skills, it was not unusual for her to misspell five words on any given review.

In the fourth grade she learned to spell, while in the third grade the teacher learned what words she already knew.

The above traditional education classroom example illustrates other problems. One problem is relevancy. For the curriculum to be living it needs to be relevant to the life and ministry of each student. Learning a list of spelling words, which are unrelated to the day-to-day activities or ministry of students, presents to them a meaningless learning experience. Educators are deceiving themselves if they believe that lists of spelling words contributed by out-of-state curriculum publishers are meaningful because they are supposed to be words appropriate to certain grade levels or to be useful in the unknown future. This type of meaning is far too abstract for primary students.

Students need not be tied to words which are supposed to be at their learning level. If students are studying a subject which excites them they will reach beyond levels which are considered normal. For example, my son, Jonathan, and many other boys in the late primary or early middle school years are interested in dinosaurs. Jonathan easily learned to spell the names of various dinosaurs while in the fourth grade because he wanted to learn them. Traditional curriculum does not provide for this. An individualized curriculum will enhance learning by making it relevant to each child's personal interests and life ministry.

Consequently, a twofold problem for traditional educators is that of deceit and theft. Some Christian school parents are deceived into thinking that their children are receiving a Christian education when their children are given spelling words to learn that they already know. In fact, this is theft, too, because tuition money has been received for a service which is not being performed. Students are being robbed of their Christian education when teachers use traditional curriculum that does not accommodate their individual needs or places them at a point in the curriculum that is inappropriate to their learning abilities. When biblical principles of student individuality are omitted, Christian schools lose a key Christian distinction and become like statist public schools.

3. Regenerate and Unregenerate

Although Christians know that God created man in His image and that this presupposition must apply to all human beings,

God has also distinguished two types of men. Both types of men must always be considered by Christian educators. There is one group of people who have been regenerated by the Holy Spirit and another group of people who have not been regenerated by the Holy Spirit - the unregenerate.[25] This supposition or belief will affect the hiring of personnel, student enrollment, curriculum development, teaching methods, and virtually every area of Christian school education. In fact, it is impossible for Christian schools to be biblically directed and not have this discrimination influence the entire educational process.

The difference between people being regenerate or unregenerate is the same difference between people being Christians in the biblical sense of having experienced "born again" salvation, and non-Christians who are not saved or "born again." There are innumerable results of this distinction which are pertinent for Christian education. For example, Christians are led by the Holy Spirit, are in submission to the authority of the Bible, and, for them, in all things Christ has preeminence. On the other hand, non-Christians are led by their own will or desires, accept the authority of science or the majority or create their own authority, and, for them, in all things self-interest has the preeminence.

Sometimes the distinction between the regenerate and unregenerate is acknowledged by Christian school leaders, but they choose not to discriminate on this principle. An illustration of this is easily identified within a Christian school's student enrollment policy. Some Christian educators believe that they should not exclude non-Christian families from enrolling their children in Christian school.[26] Usually this open enrollment policy is adopted because a strong evangelistic emphasis is incorporated within the school for the student body. In these schools, the purpose for the school's existence may be evangelism or evangelism is the primary goal or objective.

Almost always the distinction between the regenerate and unregenerate is applied to faculty hiring policies by Christian school leaders. Discriminating Christian personnel applications from non-Christian personnel applications is vital for all Christian school leaders because, "if the gospel be hidden, it is hidden to them that are lost, in whom the god of this age hath blinded the minds of unbelievers. . ." (II Cor 4:3-4). Unbelieving faculty members, therefore, have the gospel hidden to them, they have their minds blinded by false gods and, thus, are unable to "walk in the Spirit" or to shape students for "living in the Spirit" (Gal 5:16,22-25) or to teach in a Christian school.

Certainly this principle was an early teaching of the English Reformation. Robert Grosseteste was a bishop in Suffolk during the middle years of the thirteenth century. Pope Innocent commanded him to provide an unbelieving canonry to his infant nephew.

> Grosseteste replied: "After the sin of Lucifer there is none more opposed to the gospel than that which ruines souls by giving them a faithless minister. Bad pastors are the cause of unbelief, heresy, and disorder. Those who introduce them into the church [or school] are little better than antichrists."[27]

A strong statement! Applied to contemporary Christian education, it condemns the placement of covenant children under the tutelage of faithless teachers because it contributes heartily to unbelief, heresy, and disorder.

An area where the distinction between regenerate and unregenerate is seriously deficient is in the curriculum. Except for some forms of evangelism, this essential difference is not applied to learning theory, curriculum content or teaching methods. Irrespective of a school's admission policy, Christian schools have both regenerate and unregenerate student learners. But nowhere is there to be found a Christian school, two-track, educational program. Separate learning theory, teaching methods, curriculum content, and evaluation procedures need to be developed for both types of students. Unregenerate learners are "dead in trespasses and sins." They walk or learn "according to the course of this world, according to the prince of the power of the air. . . ," and have in all manner of life "the lusts of the flesh, fulfilling the desires of the flesh and of the mind," and are "by nature the children of wrath. . ." (Eph 2:1-3). Clear differentiation must be made for students whom God has made alive by grace through faith and are now "His workmanship created in Christ Jesus unto good works, which God hath before ordained that [they] should walk in them" (Eph 2:4-10). A custom-made curriculum allows for the development of this biblical differentiation, while traditional Christian curriculum does not make this biblical distinction.

The distinction allows biblical educators to avoid the problems identified by Ezekiel when he wrote about the decadence of Jerusalem. Among many offenses, he wrote that the Lord God said, "Her priests [teachers] have violated my law, and have profaned my holy things; they have put no difference between the holy and profane, neither have they shown the difference between the unclean and the clean..." (Eze 22:26). The teaching prescribed by secular educators in their curriculums claims that there is no difference, and instead of showing students the difference between right and wrong based on God's law, they encourage students to create and clarify their own values. Christian educators and students cannot be a part of this without compromising Christ.

4. Interpretation

A fundamental presupposition for Christian teaching and learning is the belief that factual content or information cannot be separated from biblical principles. In other words, basic skills and learning content can never be isolated from biblical principles of interpretation if education is to be Christian. To be sure, non-Christian principles of interpretation may be substituted for biblical principles, but basic learning skills and facts, at all times, stand in relationship to principles of interpretation. Therefore, information is never neutral but is always taught or learned in a context which gives meaning and understanding to the student. There is no "twilight zone of semi-neutrality between believers and unbelievers"[28] when it comes to interpreting facts. Every student's understanding will be in accord with God's Word or it will be out of harmony with being captive to Christ. An either-or situation exists: God's view or man's view. Facts are *always* joined with one of these two views.

Christian educators must understand that "no 'fact' is seen as it really is unless it is seen in its correct relationship to God. Since God has made the space-time facts, their relation to God is naturally the most important thing to know about them. But more than that ... that very relationship to God exhausts the meaning of the fact."[29] Thus, "the ground for the necessity of Christian schools lies in this very thing, that no fact can be known unless it be known in its relationship to God."[30] In contrast, non-Christian educators believe that "facts" can be known without being understood in relationship to God. Since God created every fact, His mark continuously appears in every fact, therefore, non-Christian educators are continuously confronted by God and they continuously oppose Him in unrighteousness (Rom 1:18-23). Their insistence on interpreting factual content apart from God means that there is no overlap or common interpretation of the facts between Christian educators and learners and non-Christian educators and learners.

Accordingly, if Christian educators fail to set forth their Christian interpretation presuppositions then Christian schools fail to distinguish Christian education from non-Christian education. Without this distinction clearly set forth, facts interpreted by the biblical perspective would be identical to facts interpreted by a non-biblical perspective. Hence essential biblical supremacy, authority and necessity are compromised in favor of the bar of human neutrality. In other words, it is "tantamount to saying that those who interpret a fact as dependent upon God and those who interpret the same fact as not dependent upon God have yet said something identical about the fact."[31] Were this true, Christian schools, churches, and in fact, all of Christianity would be unnecessary.

5. Purpose

Educators and students alike, presuppose that there is a purpose for what they are doing. Perhaps the purpose is unclear, unknown or some pie-in-the-sky ideal. Nevertheless it is assumed by people that the activities of life and school have purpose. Indeed, it is characteristic for students to ask their teachers, "Why do we have to do this?" or "What good is it?" or they may say, "Learn this? What for?" Thus, like the ancient Greeks, students still ask, "What is the purpose of life?" They want to know what, for man is the highest good or the summum bonum.

There is a clear difference between the Christian educator's purpose in learning and the non-Christian educator's purpose in learning. The Christian educator knows that God has an ultimate purpose for all that He created and for all that takes place. It is God's purpose for His creation that underlies the Christian educator's purpose and it gives meaning to the student's learning of factual content and skills.

For example, as we provide computers for our children, we must remember that our students are being prepared for biblical service-living in the natural world. There must be excellence in providing them with computer skills. They must willingly acknowledge God by ascribing to Him the glory for each skill. Covenant students must see themselves as laborers worthy of His hire; conscientious, honest, loyal, and righteous. God is glorified and His purpose is fulfilled as these and other skills are put into Christian service and not by mere intellectual assent to God's glory. "For we are laborers together with God; ye are God's husbandry, God's building . . . for other foundation [Christ's purpose] can no man lay than that which is laid, which is Jesus Christ" (I Cor 3:9-11). In contrast, the non-Christian's purpose or highest good is self-serving, worldly or materialistic. Non-Christian educators and learners do not ever purpose with Scripture's directive, which says, "whatever you do [purpose], whether in word or deed, do [purpose] it all in the name of the Lord Jesus, giving thanks to God the Father through Him" (Col 3:17).

Christian educators and learners, therefore, believe that learning and all good works must be done to the glory of God. This means that Christian school leaders will adopt God's plan, program, highest good, purpose, or will as their own and will concentrate their powers in order to consciously implement the plan God has set. Accordingly, Christian students must "will to will the will of God for the whole world . . . ."[32] The idea is for them to set their highest goal to be perfect in correspondence to God's perfect plan. In short, the chief end of Christian education is to glorify God and to enable His followers to enjoy Him forever. It is to fulfill the dominion mandate (Gen 1:26).

It should be noted by Christian educators and parents that the purpose or the highest good of Christian education is not simply acknowledging God for the glory of God. It is more than recognizing or appreciating that God has something to do with whatever is being learned. Certainly it is indisputable that the relationship between God and each part of His creation is important. But it is equally important to accompany this Christian understanding with performing actual Christian ministry. Without ministry accompanying Christian education, Christian education is reduced to being a daydream or a platonic fantasy. Christian ministry and service must become an integral part of Christian school education in order for Christian schools, educators, and learners to understand God's highest good and to fulfill God's purpose for creation.

6. Ministry

The Bible teaches that Christians, including children or students "must learn to devote themselves to doing what is good, in order that they may provide for daily necessities and not live unproductive lives" (Titus 3:14). This means that both adults and children are to perform good works which, in part, provide for the essentials of daily living. Further, the Scripture tells of "things that accompany salvation." "God is not unjust; He will not forget your work and the love that you have shown Him as you have helped His people and continued to help them" (Hebrews 6:9-12). Without a shadow of a doubt, associated with salvation is the Lord's promise to remember all the service and ministry that Christians perform for one another in the name of the Lord God. At the same time the Lord says to His people, "be not slothful" (Heb 6:12).

These teachings become the ministry presupposition for Christian school educators. It is expected by Christian educators and parents that every Christian student is being educationally prepared to live a life of service unto the Lord. In fact, Jesus taught that Christians in general, particularly teachers, are not to be like non-Christians and "lord over" or "exercise authority over" others. Rather, He said that "whosoever wants to be great among [Christians] is to be their minister and whosoever is to be chief among [Christians] is to be their servant; for [Christians] are to be like Christ Who came to serve and give His life a ransom for many" (Matt 20:25-28 NASV).

This concept is unknown to non-Christian educators. It is not incorporated in statist public schools by Christian teachers. In brief, non-Christian educators and students are out to serve their own self interests. They may be claiming to serve all of humanity but actually they are a part of humanity and are, thus, ultimately serving themselves. Certainly, they do not follow the Lord's command when He says, "Thou shalt fear the Lord Thy God and serve Him . . ." nor do they pursue God's charge to Solomon, through David, when He says "know thou the God of thy father, and serve Him with a perfect heart and with a willing mind;" (I Cor 28:9). No one can serve two masters, so, with Joshua all people must choose whom they will serve; the Lord

God of the Scriptures or other gods. Those who fear the Lord will in the future see the results of their choice when the Lord discerns "between the righteous and the wicked, between him that serveth God and him that serveth Him not" (Mal 3:18).

Unfortunately, this ministry concept is known but undeveloped by Christian educators. It is not too much to say that Christian educators know about the Lord's gold mine of Christian ministry for student-learners but have yet to begin the mining operations. Certainly there has been much talking and some writing about this heavenly treasure but actual learning ministries have been limited to a few traditional samples; Christmas programs, services held at the city mission, or an athletic testimony. These are good, but are only a few samples of what remain to be unearthed from the Lord's unlimited treasures of ministry. Tendency learning, that is, "learning in which a student acquires tendencies to action"[33] is a positive step but it does not go far enough. It must be more than just "to aim at inducting students into or training them for a Christian *way of life*; [it must do more than to] . . . point towards living the Christian life, in obedience, as agents of God's cause in the world."[34] Christian learning must include covenant students actually *being* the Lord's ministers. Jay Adams has begun to uncover this hidden treasure with his *Ministering Projects* idea.[35] Also, Geraldine J. Steensma and Harro W. Brummelen have promoted this ministry concept with their ideas of student practicums for social concerns.[36]

Christian schools ought to be hubs for Christian student ministries. They should always reflect the biblical ministry presupposition by actively guiding students in *being* Christian ministers and servants rather than only abstractly preparing students for a *future of doing* Christian ministry. The reality is that Christian students are only receiving a genuine Christian education when they are learning skills and factual content in relationship to God by implementing them in the *immediate* purpose of *actively using* them in service or ministry to the Lord. Learning in the Christian schema is not simply learning for learning's sake. Christian learning is to glorify God and this means that learning is relevant to the present and that learning is to *be* a ministry by implementing the learned material into the real world as a genuine service or help.

7. Christian Education: A Great Antithesis

The difference between Christian education and non-Christian education is total. They are completely opposed to each other in every respect. They are two distinct forms of education. Ultimately, they are not the same in any way. The distinction between the Christian and non-Christian presuppositions illustrates that the contrast or the antithesis is all-comprehensive. "Every Christian educator should come to grips with this point. And anyone who comes to grips with it at all will sense the impossibility of thinking of Christian education as being ninety or sixty or thirty or ten percent like other education. . . . When viewed from this standpoint then, Christian education is not even a fraction of one percent like public education."[37] In short, "the different conceptions of God that underlie the two educational theories cover every front on the whole front."[38]

At the outset, it should be made clear that both Christian and non-Christian educators share use of the same information, facts, and relate to the world using the same skills. For example, typing skills are the same for both, and both share the things of God's creation: water, land, numbers, food, colors, sunshine, etc. This is part of God's common grace. Nevertheless, the things which appear alike are ultimately different in the areas of learning, understanding and purpose. Whenever a Christian educator or learner interacts with any bit of information or with a skill, this interaction is altogether different because of the biblical presuppositions which direct their minds. Non-Christian educators may attempt with all their powers to be "objective" or unprejudiced or indiscriminatory but the Bible teaches that in all their ways non-Christians are corrupt; thus, their presumption that there is no God disfigures all their thinking. On the other hand, Christian educators consciously purpose to design all of their thinking with a bias that the God of the Bible is the author and the finisher of all education. No intermediate position exists. Synthesis of the two is inconceivable and utterly impossible. The Christian world- and life-view, the "Christian way of life"[39] is in complete and absolute antithesis to all non-Christian world- and life-views or ways of life.

Christian school leaders should also know that for non-Christian educators there is no antithesis, since non-Christians do not affirm an infinite personal God, the Creator, who is in all respects distinct from creation. They assume that all reality is ultimately non-personal and, thus, materialistic. For non-Christians, all the diverse parts of the universe including what some people call god are evolving together in combination or synthesis. Christian educators and students, in contrast, must always maintain the distinction between the Creator God and His creation. Accordingly, Christian educators must implement, in all areas, the corresponding implications of this distinction. The story of Adam and Eve provides an excellent illustration. Before they ate of the fruit they had an opportunity to choose between obeying God's command or not obeying it. The choice presents an antithesis. They chose against God; consequently all men, apart from God's redeeming grace, in every thought and deed always choose against God. There is no other choice, for fallen mankind is dead in sin. Accordingly, it was not long after the Fall that everyone, save Noah by grace, assumed that there was no God. Since God was not a part of their thinking, they could only choose not to obey God. All choices are ultimately the same for those who reject God and these common choices tend to join together as a whole in synthesis against God. Those who assume there is no God have their own standards which are not authoritative and are always changing; while those who begin with God in their thinking realize that God's absolute standard stands in continuous opposition to all other relative standards.

Christian educators must be certain that the distinction or antithesis between Godly learning activity and a non-Christian's ungodly learning activity is always a part of the student's learning experience. It is good for Christian learners to consciously understand the contrast between their thinking God's thoughts after God within a given learning experience from those who reject God's thoughts. We are not out to shelter covenant students from the realities of the world. It is the secular public or private schools that shelter students from the realities of God's truth. Understanding this contrast will enable covenant students to know, like the people before Joshua, that they choose the Lord and they will then be able to say, "God forbid that we should forsake the Lord to serve other gods; . . . Nay, but we will serve the Lord. The Lord our God will we serve, and His voice will we obey" (Josh 24:14-24).

In addition, covenant students will then understand and

comprehend with true appreciation the promises of God. With these promises, they will comprehend their covenant responsibilities. God's children will be taught not to squander the wealth, the inheritance or the grace of God. They will be taught to apply the treasured talents the Lord has given rather than let them lie idle.[40] Furthermore, they will know that "faith is required in the children of the covenant" to believe in Jesus Christ unto salvation, to turn from sin to holiness and to "follow the highway of sanctification through life."[41] This faith is indispensable and it is imperative that it not "be a bare intellectual assent to the claims of Christ nor a mere stirring of emotions resulting from an impassioned plea nor, finally, a momentary impulsive choice under high psychological pressure. It must be a deliberate response of the heart that is deeply conscious of sin to the glorious offer of salvation in Christ; the 'amen' of the soul elicited by the Holy Spirit to all the blessed promises of the Gospel; the hearty and unqualified acceptance of all the covenant obligations."[42]

It is good that creation is taught in contrast to evolution at most Christian schools. They are not to be debated as if biblical truth were a mere scientific hypothesis. There is also value when private secular or statist public schools teach this distinction. Public school curriculum does not include the teaching that creation is absolutely true, so they invariably teach in an accommodating or compromising manner. Notwithstanding, the antithesis teaching cannot be limited to this or a few other isolated issues. Every issue, every fact, every teaching is involved in the war between Christ and Satan. "It is the nature of the conflict between Christ and Satan to be all-comprehensive."[43] The antithesis is everywhere and Christian teachers are responsible to point it out to their students. Christian learners ought to be able to examine a salt shaker on the kitchen table, an amoeba under the microscope, a cartoon in the newspaper, or a musical instrument being played at a concert with penetrating insight into the antithesis between intricate involvement with God's interpretation of the object and fraudulent involvement with godless interpretation of the object. To be sure, this antithesis can be taught to some degree to very young children as they develop an understanding of biblical righteousness in contrast to unbiblical behavior.

8. Christian Education: A Definition

The concept called, "Christian education," is not always clearly defined. Some Christian educators give definitions that are not distinctly biblical because the biblical interpreting principles are assumed and are not directly evident in the definition.[44] Such definitions are weak because non-Christian educators may readily use them by applying their own non-Christian presuppositions. Other Christian educators do not provide a concise definition; instead, they prefer to develop written chapters which point out "norms and objectives for Christian education"[45] or biblical principles.[46] These chapters are good for expanded study; however a brief definition is not given.

Three succinct definitions of Christian education are:

1. "Christian education is education aimed at training for the Christian way of life."[47]

2. Christian education is "nurturing the development of God's life within believers."[48]

3. Christian "education is implication into God's interpretation."[49]

Another crisp definition is: *Christian education is the Spirit-formed actualization of biblical Christianity throughout the teaching-learning-ministry process of each covenant student.* This definition provides keys for advancing the concept of Christian education and improving the Christian educational process. The chief principles in this definition are: (1) the Spirit of God does the forming, shaping and educating; (2) it is biblical Christianity that Christian educators are to be purposely promoting; (3) the Christian way of life is to be actually carried out in the present through each student's learning activities, not reduced to being a step of training for the future; (4) learning is to be an active, service-oriented, Godly ministry that goes beyond the platonic ideal of knowledge for knowledge's sake; and (5) the teaching-learning process must be thoroughly biblical including procedures and experience-activities.

The definition given of Christian education and the five principles listed are not a part of public school education. In fact, public school educators never promote this definition of Christian education. Accordingly, Christian educators ought not pattern Christian schools after public schools.

Christian schools must be reconstructed according to biblical principles. The whole Christian system of education must follow the plans drawn by the Master Architect. A reformation is in order for Christian schools! Until now, most Christian school leaders have taken the secular, educational system and enhanced it with Christian character and efficiency but have kept the humanist substructure. Furthermore, the humanist substructure has deeply influenced administrative procedures, teaching methods, curriculum design, daily class scheduling, record keeping, classroom appearance, evaluations at every level, building construction, fund-raising, lesson plans and a host of other school functions. This influence must be removed.

In other words, God's school system is founded upon God's covenant and is to be built entirely with biblical precepts. The reformers of the sixteenth century called for this to be applied to God's church system. A clear contrast was established by the reformers. They separated from the way of life perpetuated by the Renaissance humanists and protested against the abuses of the Roman Catholic church. Luther wanted to remain within the church in order to direct teaching into being biblical teaching but Lutherans after him and other Protestants withdrew from the established church because of its refusal to biblically reform. "Sola Scriptura" was their claim. Today's Christian school reformers are facing the same conflicts with modern, secular humanism and with the humanistic practices which are unwittingly being exercised within Christian schools and associations of Christian schools. Hopefully, a clear line of demarcation will be established and maintained between today's secular humanists in contrast to biblical, Christian education and that another division within Christian school groups will be unnecessary. "To deny God in one point is to attack God in all."[50]

9. The Holy Spirit: The Christian's Educator

The Holy Spirit holds a central place in biblical Christian education. Christian schools readily affirm their belief in the third Person of the Trinity. However, when curriculum guides, lesson plans, textbooks, and the teaching-learning process are examined there is little or no mention of the Holy Spirit. It seems that the Holy Spirit's place is abstractly programmed to morning devotions, chapel services, or Bible classes but is virtually non-existent during the rest of the school day.

The Bible says that the Holy Spirit has a major role in learning. It says that God has prepared special things to be learned for those who love Him. "God has revealed them unto us by His Spirit; for the Spirit searcheth all things, yea, the deep things of God. . . . Now we [Christians] have received, not the spirit of the world, but the Spirit who is of God. . . . [Christians are not taught words in human wisdom but are taught by the wisdom of the Holy Spirit]" (I Cor 2:9-13). Thus, there is no doubt that the Holy Spirit is the Christian's master teacher. To be sure, Jesus is our example and it is the words of Christ that Christians are to learn, but ultimately, it is the Spirit of God who triggers learning; who grants Godly understanding. Human teachers are to proclaim the Word of God; they are to model it in biblical Christian living and, hence, they can prepare receptive hearts for the wisdom taught by the Holy Spirit. They cannot force the gift of learning or appropriate the grace of Almighty God. The Lord works through educators who plant and water the minds of covenant students with the full counsel of God's word; yet, it is God who causes the growth, the learning, and who gives the wisdom.

Genuine Christian education is nothing less than biblical sanctification, that is, Christian growth. "Christian education depends on the Spirit's illumination and application of His book, the Bible, for the correct perception and relationship of every fact, and on His energizing power for living according to biblical truth in all aspects of life."[51] Christian education, therefore, is *always* religious, *always* moral, *always* active service, *always* in harmony with the Bible, and *always* powered by the work of the Holy Spirit. Both sanctification and biblical learning are alone the work of the Holy Spirit.

The indispensable work of the Holy Spirit was a major element acknowledged by the reformers. Thomas Bilney, a young student at Cambridge in the early sixteenth century, asked in response to a priest of popery, "What would be the use of being a hundred times consecrated, were it even by a thousand papal bulls if the inward calling is wanting? To no purpose hath the bishop breathed on our hands if we have never felt the breath of the Holy Ghost in our hearts?" Certainly, the reformers knew and attested to the essential role of the Holy Spirit in learning. They proclaimed that it was men whom God anointed with His Spirit who were teachers of the truth while the Roman hierarchy feared the baptism of the Holy Ghost perfected by the faith in the Word of God.[52]

10. The Holy Spirit Initiates Christian Education

Adams believes that "it is fair to say that Christian education truly begins for a student only when he is saved: 'the fear of the Lord is the beginning of wisdom.'"[53] God affirms this with several clear analogies. Before people are saved, they are described as being "dead"; after receiving the gift of salvation, they are described as "those made alive from the dead" (Rom 6:11-13). Other analogies are: darkness becoming light, evil with being good, blindness with receiving sight, lost with being found and sickness with being made well. Certainly an all-comprehensive transformation of the mind takes place when the Holy Spirit regenerates those whom the Lord has called unto Himself. The Christian's mind is "born again." Christian students set their minds according to the things of the Spirit while non-Christian students set their minds on the things of the flesh (Rom 8:5-8). A complete metamorphosis, like the change of a caterpillar into a beautiful butterfly, transfigures the new Christian's way of learning and living. The Holy Spirit performs this change. The change is from one which is "in the vanity of their mind, having the understanding darkened, being alienated from the life of God through the ignorance that is in them, because of the blindness of their heart" (Eph 4:17-18) into people who "walk circumspectly ... redeeming the time ... understanding what the will of the Lord is" (Eph 5:15-17). Consequently, when a person is converted to biblical Christianity by the Spirit of God, the conversion begins a new way of life which includes a new way of learning and thinking that is God-conscious and is no longer at war with God.

11. The Holy Spirit Activates the Christian Mind

"The Holy Spirit is concerned in the formation of the human mind and the unfolding of the spirit of humanity."[54] Furthermore, "human nature is adapted in creation to the inworking of the Holy Spirit, without which it cannot unfold itself any more than the rosebud without light and the influence of the sun. As the ear cannot hear without sound, and the eye cannot see without light, so is our human nature incomplete without the light and indwelling of the Spirit."[55] In other words, God created the mind of man to be in constant communion with the Father through the work of the Holy Spirit. Sin destroyed this communion. Man was created to operate in fellowship with the Spirit of God for the glory of God. When this fellowship was broken by sin, the mind of man ceased to operate correctly. The power pack was removed from him because sinful man preferred self-controlled, manual operation. His depraved mind is reactivated solely by the regenerating power of the Holy Spirit. When the mind of fallen man is powered by the regenerating work of the Spirit of God, man's true humanity is unfolded as God created it to operate, in fellowship with Him.

"And the Lord spoke to Moses, saying, see, I have called by name Bezalel, ... I have filled Him with the Spirit of God, in wisdom, and in understanding, and in knowledge, and in all manner of workmanship.... In the hearts of all that are wisehearted I have put wisdom, that they may make all that I have commanded them" (Ex 31:1,3,6). Accordingly, it is clear that the Lord works directly through His Spirit to enable men who are filled with the Spirit to comprehend Himself and to skillfully apply this understanding to their workmanship. Unregenerate men, in contrast, do not have this "wisdom," "understanding," "knowledge," and "manner of workmanship" because they unceasingly suppress the Spirit of God in unrighteousness (Rom 1:18).

To be sure, unregenerate men have excellent artistic skills and talents. Apart from the Spirit's gift of regenerating grace, the Spirit does bestow personal talent upon unregenerate men as part of His common grace to all men for the ultimate glory of God. Nonetheless, all unregenerate men exchange the biblical manner of workmanship in truth, knowledge, and wisdom for a lie; they glorify Him not as God; neither are they thankful, for they are vain and foolish, and they worship and serve the creature rather than the Creator (Rom 1:21-25). Consequently, in contrast to regenerate learners, unregenerate learners never acknowledge the necessary and rightful role of the Holy Spirit in the teaching-learning process. Without His role being given priority, biblical learning is always voided.

Regenerate learners have been "sealed with that Holy Spirit of promise" (Eph 1:13). These learners are no longer "strangers from the covenants of promise" (Eph 2:11), but actively build their minds and lives "upon the foundation of the apostles and prophets, Jesus Christ Himself being the chief cornerstone" (Eph 2:20). Accordingly, it is clear that the Holy Spirit is integral to God's covenant from its first administration with Adam through its final administration with Christ. Paul tells us that the Spirit has revealed to believers the mystery of Christ and has graciously given understanding and knowledge which is not known to unregenerate learners. It is the same Spirit of God which revealed the grace of God to the prophets in the old administration of the covenant who also revealed further revelation of the grace of God to the apostles under Christ's administration of God's covenant (Eph 3:1-5).

Therefore, the connection between the covenant foundations for Christian education which were demonstrated in Part I of this book, and the principles for Christian education in Part II are established by the Spirit of promise. The Spirit of God is the regenerating Agent for God's everlasting covenant in the lives of regenerate men and He is the same Agent who transforms the minds and actions of regenerate learners into conformity with biblical teaching. It is the promised transformation which the Holy Spirit actively performs in the perfection of the saints: "That in every work effected by Father, Son, and Holy Ghost in common, the power to bring forth proceeds from the Father; the power to arrange from the Son; the power to perfect from the Holy Spirit."[56] Consequently we stand with Paul saying that we are "confident of this very thing, that He who began a good work in you will perfect it until the day of Christ Jesus" (Phil 1:6). "To make perfect, is the proper work of the Holy Spirit"[57] and it is this Spirit which works in an enlightened way in the teaching-learning process with regenerate learners while He remains a mystery to all unregenerate educators.

12. The Holy Spirit's Role in the Learning Process

The Holy Spirit's perfecting of the minds and lives of regenerate learners is illustrated in the following model.

MODEL 1
Part A

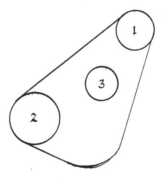

unregenerate man
attempts to power
the drive belt to
gain wisdom and
understanding

1. Unregenerate learners — thinking and living in sin; suppressing God in total unrighteousness.

2. Knowledge of the universe that is fleshly and thus is acquired in this condition by the mind of the learner.

3. Knowledge of the universe which is innate or within the learner from conception; knowledge of God which God placed within every man and wrote upon his heart.

Part B

Holy Spirit engages and drives belt

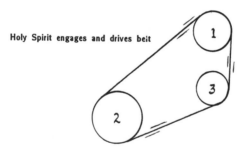

Regenerate learners are
powered by the
Holy Spirit and
thus wisdom and
understanding are obtained

1. Regenerate learners — thinking and living in Christ's imputed righteousness; submitting to God consciously.

2. Knowledge of the universe that is biblical and thus is acquired in this condition by the mind of the learner.

3. Activated knowledge of the universe which is innate or within the learner from conception; Spirit—illuminated knowledge of God which reveals from God that which God placed within every man and wrote upon his heart.

Model 1 is patterned after the concept of a belt-driven engine. Part A illustrates the unregenerate learner. This learner suppresses the Holy Spirit; thus, the belt drive is never engaged. Since the drive belt is never engaged, the knowledge of the universe is fleshly and is never truly or rightly acquired. Certainly, the unregenerate learner is in contact with the knowledge of the universe but his drive belt is spinning under his own power which is insufficient to acquire truth, understanding or the glory of God. The drive belt is connected so that the unregenerate learner is able to function in God's universe but because the Spirit of God has not brought regeneration this learner is "ever learning, and never able to come to the knowledge of the truth" (II Tim 3:7). The same is true of unregenerate teachers and applies to all of their teachings.

In contrast, Part B shows the drive belt that is engaged by the Holy Spirit. The innate knowledge of the universe is brought into contact with newly acquired biblical knowledge by the Spirit of God. Only the Spirit of God is able to release the innate knowledge which God has written on the hearts of men. When the Spirit regenerates a learner He engages God's covenant and releases God-conscious thinking and activity on the part of the learner. "I will give them one heart, and I will put a new spirit within you" (Ez 11:19); "This is the covenant that I will make with them after those days, saith the Lord: I will put my laws into their hearts, and in their minds will I write them" (Heb 10:16; 8:10; Jer 31:31-34). Clearly, the wrath of God and that which is known about God is evident within unregenerate men, for God made it evident to them, but they completely and continuously suppress the truth (Rom 1:18-21). Yet once the Holy Spirit is within, the stony heart is exchanged for a heart of flesh (Ez 11:19). Hence the regenerate learner is able to walk in God's statutes and keep His ordinances. He is able to do this because the Word of God that was written on his heart is no longer suppressed but is released and warmly embraced. In other words, the Holy Spirit is the agent who works on the hearts and minds of regenerate learners in order to establish a union between God's natural revelation which is acquired from without and the innate law of God written on their hearts. These forms of natural revelation are completely in accord with God's revelation in Scripture. In fact, together they "form God's one grand scheme of covenant revelation of Himself to man. The two forms of revelation must therefore be seen as presupposing and supplementing one another"[58] under the constant power and direction of the Holy Spirit. There is no alternative except to "quench" the Spirit (I Thes 5:19).

According to the above model, the Holy Spirit is the true, teaching agent. He is the One who enlightens the mind. Learning is not based on some type of acquired knowledge. In fact, Scripture teaches that "Eye hath not seen, nor ear heard, neither have entered into the heart of man, the things which God hath prepared for them that love Him. But God hath revealed them unto us by His spirit" (I Cor 3:9). Clearly, it is God's Spirit who works from within the learner to release the law of God written on the heart and to knit the union of this law with the acquired knowledge about the created universe and Scripture. To be sure, a union is always made by man in rebellion to God or by the Spirit of God within man. Man's autonomous learning, however, is always false and blasphemous because it denies the Creator while the Spirit's revelation is always true and honoring to God Almighty.

It is amazing that Christian educators have ignored the Spirit's essential role in the teaching-learning process. Entire textbooks, workbooks, and most Christian teacher conferences have neglected to include the Holy Spirit as life-supporting for learning. Why are there no workshops which enhance an understanding of the Spirit's work in the hearts and lives of students? Why have textbook and curriculum publishers assumed that biblical, Spirit given learning will take place if the teacher follows a prescribed step-by-step process while not clearly proclaiming the Spirit's workmanship?

At the Continental Congress on the Christian World View II, an outstanding assemblage of Christian leaders met together. Representing the church, home and school, they wrote an educational document" which was to be presented to the world as representing the educational essentials of the "Christian World View" for Christian education. This amazing document included sections on "Freedom of Inquiry," "The Beginning," "Human Condition," "Life Ethics," "The Social Good," "Life Psychology," and "Sexuality" but not one word on the place of the Holy Spirit in Christian education. We were warned against the infiltration of socialism, Naziism, and communism. It was affirmed that any education worthy of our time should be based upon biblical economics, politics, and morals. Yet, I ask, how can any education worthy of the name Christian ignore the indispensable Spirit of God? Unfortunately, even in the center of many Christian circles, the Holy Spirit remains entirely mystical and reference to Him is limited to brief acknowledgements of the reality of His existence or power. This is all too true of Christian schools.

Acknowledgement of the Holy Spirit is life-giving for Christian educators and regenerate learners. Education is made alive by the Spirit of God. "What air is to man's physical nature, the Holy Spirit is to his spiritual nature. Without air there is death in our bodies; without the Holy Spirit there is death in our souls."[59] The same is true of education; without the Holy Spirit there is death in our educational system and in the entire teaching-learning process. Secularists detest this view and are openly hostile while true biblical educators passionately embrace the Spirit of God in all of their activities. Unfortunately, all too few work out the educational implications of this embrace.

Education cannot unfold itself into truth, learning, wisdom, knowledge, service or understanding without the light and direction of the Holy Spirit. As the computer cannot compute without a program, and the video cannot be seen without a monitor, so human learning is extinguished without the light and indwelling of the Spirit.

13. Specific Educational Works of the Holy Spirit

To discuss the specific works of the Holy Spirit we must first acknowledge His regenerating service. This is clearly revealed to us in Scripture and summarized in question 65 of the Heidelberg Catechism, which says:

> Q. You confess, that by faith alone you share in Christ and all His blessings: where does that faith come from?
> A. The Holy Spirit produces it in our hearts by the preaching of the holy gospel."
> (I John 3:5; I Cor 2:10-14; Eph 2:8; Rom 10:17; I Pet 1:23-25.)

It is upon this regenerating foundation, constructed by the Holy Spirit, that the Spirit builds the minds and lives of regenerated learners. There can be no omitting of this gift of grace, the gift of salvation, for biblical learning to rightfully develop.

* * * * *

David asks, "Whither shall I go from Thy Spirit? Or whither shall I flee from Thy presence?" (Psalms 139:7.) He states positively that omnipresence belongs to the Holy Spirit.[60] In other words, the Spirit of God is always present in space and certainly in every classroom. We also know that the Holy Spirit does not dwell in every human soul. He does indwell those who have been regenerated (Rom 8:10-11). Therefore, "the Holy Spirit seems to act upon a human being in a twofold manner - from without, or from within."[61]

From without, the Spirit gives many different gifts and talents to all people. Gifts which evidence the Spirit's work from without are: Samson's strength, Joshua's military genius, or Paul's tentmaking. In educational terms the Spirit gives to some students artistic talent while others receive musical skill, mechanical or technical efficiency or cognitive competency. Nevertheless, these works of the Holy Spirit are only outward and temporal. They, in and of themselves, do not touch the spiritual realm. In contrast, the inward operation of the Spirit begins with saving grace and then proceeds to perpetuate its continuous and everlasting activity within the spirit of each believer. The inward activity of the Holy Spirit includes bringing forth a desire to keep the laws and statutes of God. It transforms the Spirit's work from within to incorporate the Spirit's work from without. In other words, the inward work of the Spirit is able to take the Spirit-given works from without and to actualize them in ways that are eternal, righteous, and actively in the service of God for the glory of God. The essential interlock of the inward work of the Holy Spirit with His external work is critical for biblical Christian educational systems. Without it they are limited to the outward work of God's Spirit like all non-Christians and their school systems.

The knowledge which God reveals to His regenerate learners through the Spirit of God is unique and completely different from worldly knowledge. "But the knowledge which is peculiar to saving faith is of a special kind," writes Bavinck. "It is not purely a theoretical knowledge, taken up solely in the mind and memory. . . . The knowledge of faith is a practical knowledge, a knowledge of the heart rather than the head, a knowledge with a personal, profound, soul-absorbing concern, for it pertains to something which my existence, my life, my soul, my salvation is involved."[62] This knowledge from the Holy Spirit, thus, is eternal as it involves the Christian student's eternal salvation. Moreover, with this connection, the Christian student's learning has valid meaning because the validity rests entirely with God. Validity for knowledge and truth is not simply a probability statistic, a product of reason, or "systematic consistency."[63] Christian students have far exceeded the prominent secular philosophers of the Vienna circle. These men could not find a verification principle for knowledge or truth; hence, they could not substantiate any valid meaning for their learning or life. On the other hand, Christian students have valid knowledge and truth because it is completely based upon God's written revelation and the enlightenment provided by God's Spirit working on the heart and soul.

Furthermore, as Bavinck notes, this valid knowledge is "practical knowledge." In other words, knowledge which is graciously given by the Spirit of God is carried out in real life ministry and service for the glory of God. It is not "purely theoretical knowledge, taken up solely in the mind and memory, which leaves man [students] cold and indifferent."[64] The Holy Spirit actualizes Himself from both within and without in each regenerate learner. First, He changes the heart and second, He changes the outward learning activities and enables them to become used as viable ministry activities. He takes the learning skills, course contents, or the "tools" of learning and activates them for His glory through actual ministries in the lives of each covenant student.

Calvin affirms the specific work of the Holy Spirit in directing the educational use of human reason.[65] He says, "that the reason of our mind, wherever it may turn, is miserably subject to vanity. . . . The eyes of the mind, unless the Lord open them, remain closed."[66] Moreover, the students' dependence upon the Spirit of God is a continuing progress and increase. Scripture does not teach "that our minds are illumined only for one day and that they may thereafter see of themselves." writes Calvin. The regenerate student needs "continual direction at every moment, lest He decline from the knowledge with which he has been endowed."[67] The Holy Spirit's work within the teaching-learning process is a constant work of God upon the minds of students and in the activities of life. "We cease not to pray for you and to ask that you may be filled with the knowledge of

God in all spiritual wisdom and understanding in order that you may walk worthily before God," (Col 1:9-10; Phil 1:9). When a student walks worthily before God it is by the power of the Spirit of God and it is observable in the real world of people and culture.

For the Christian teacher and student this means that the teaching-learning process is immersed from within and without by the Holy Spirit. Christian teachers and students do not add or integrate the Spirit into their lesson or work. Rather, they desire to submit in an active and obedient way to the continuous work of the Spirit which is already fully integral to all of the Christian student's life. They attempt to recognize the progressive work of the Spirit by consciously turning their minds towards Him, thereby eliminating thoughts, lessons or activities which suppress, quench or grieve Him. In this way Christian learners increase "in wisdom and stature, and in favor with God and man," like young Jesus (Luke 2:52). It should not amaze us to find Spirit-directed students astonishing teachers with their "understanding and answers" (Luke 2:46-47).

The work of the Holy Spirit is not an activity that is directly observed, such as watching a teacher instructing students with new skills, concepts or experiences. The teaching by the Spirit of God is not revealed by scientific methods or empirical research. Christian educators and parents do not acknowledge the Spirit's work through some special testing. They cannot command the Spirit to do specific teaching tasks or use some unique teaching method which insures that a distinctive is given by Him. Rather, the work of the Holy Spirit upon our students is indirectly reflected in a demonstrated God-consciousness and biblical awareness. Although we cannot see the Spirit's actual involvement in the teaching-learning process, His effect will be clearly evident by the lives of His students. For example, like the reformers, there will be a specific Spirit-consciousness about their thinking and acting. In reading the reformers we frequently see distinct references to the Spirit: "felt the breath of the Holy Ghost in our hearts, ... The Holy Ghost had not, however, been much attended to in the business, ... having God altogether before our eyes. ... A more excellent master than those doctors - the Holy Spirit speaking in Scripture - was soon to teach him a science which is not in the power of man to impart"[68] are a few illustrations. In similar manner, our children will be continuously tuned in to both the inward and outward work of the Holy Spirit. Verbally they will seek the Spirit's direction; they will readily acknowledge His work in their daily activities; and a dependence upon Him will be displayed on a regular basis by Spirit-minded students.

It is true that some students may trick their teachers and parents by masking their speech and activities with pretended Spirit-consciousness. Christian leaders can be fooled by displays, a Bible reading, sessions of prayerfulness, and the sprinkling of God words. On the other hand, students who truly desire Spirit-consciousness do sin and thereby may display a lack of Spirit direction. Nevertheless, as Christian educators, we must look to the long-term inward working of God's Spirit in the hearts of our students to set forth His outward activity in both word and deed. Teachers and pastors who constantly exhibit and orally communicate a Spirit-consciousness to students will, through the power of Scripture, be used by the Holy Spirit to perpetuate souls which are consciously yielding to Him. The true inward working of the Holy Spirit will be outwardly revealed by students. Testimony will be given to the Spirit's work by sustained Bible reading and prayer, by the consistent application of biblical principles, by a life which is Christlike, and by specific acts of ministry or service rendered for the glory of God. It will be verbalized with clear words to the glory of God. Christian school classrooms should have these biblical characteristics abundantly manifested by teachers and students.

The work of the Holy Spirit ought to be readily acknowledged in directing students to comprehend the sharp, all-inclusive distinction or antithesis between biblical and non-biblical understanding. "Thus saith the Lord, 'Learn not the way of nations'," (Jer 10:2); and Jesus further said, "Thou art an offense unto me; for you are mindful not of the things that are of God, but those that are of men" (Matt 16:23). Consequently, the Bible teaches a clear and absolute contrast between worldly or humanistic thinking and thinking which is mindful of the things of God. Paul says that Demas had forsaken him "having loved this present world" (II Tim 4:10). It is the Holy Spirit who opens the eyes of the mind which enables covenant students to understand and hold the thinking and the loving of this present world in absolute antithesis to biblical thinking. "Thus saith the Lord, . . . 'But let him that glorieth in this, that he understand and know Me, that I am the Lord who exerciseth loving kindness, justice and righteousness in the earth; for in these things I delight"' (Jer 9:23-24). Only a Spirit-given biblical education seeks to enhance a glorious understanding and knowledge of God Almighty and thus, is the Lord's delight.

On the contrary, secular schools, curriculum and personnel are "dead in their trespasses and sins" (Eph 2:1; Col 2:13) and are not delightful to the Lord. They substitute "The gods that have not made the heavens and the earth" (Jer 10:12) for the living God of Scripture. The Holy Spirit is not a vital part of the public school system. Horace Mann who championed the centralization of statist public schools did not believe in the Holy Trinity. Consequently the Spirit of God was not guiding him in his campaign to centralize public instruction. I know of no prominent public school leader in the history of modern public schools (1830 to 1987) who mightily proclaimed the work of God's Spirit. Further, Scripture says that "Every man is stupid or senseless and without knowledge. . . ." and we know "that the way of man is not in himself; it is not for man to direct his steps" (Jer 10:14,23). It is God, by His Spirit, who is to direct the steps of covenant children by exchanging their independent stupidity for minds captivated by the mind of Christ. This stark contrast is made throughout biblical education as a result of the specific work of the Holy Spirit. "It is not man, but God, who makes the distinction here."[69]

To summarize the concrete work of the Holy Spirit in biblical education, Kuyper's words are to the point.

> The sanctification [the biblical education and life ministry] of the human consciousness is wrought in us by God in a divine, unfathomable and irresistible way; but not independently of the Word, for that Word is itself divine, and the preaching [teaching] can only present the matter to the consciousness, it is the Holy Ghost who makes the heart understand it, declares it to the consciousness, works conviction, and causes the consciousness to assent to it, and thus enables it to feel the pressure which proceeds from that which is written on the heart.[70]

NOTES

1. Cornelius Van Til CHRISTIAN THEISTIC ETHICS (Nutley, N.J.: Presbyterian and Reformed Publishing Company, 1977) p.179.

2. Ibid., p.195.

3. Jay Adams BACK TO THE BLACKBOARD, p.69.

4. Robert L. Reymond THE JUSTIFICATION OF KNOWLEDGE: AN INTRODUCTORY STUDY IN CHRISTIAN APOLOGETIC METHODOLOGY (Phillipsburg, N.J.: Presbyterian and Reformed Publishing Company, 1979) p.8.

5. Cornelius Van Til A SURVEY OF CHRISTIAN EPISTEMOLOGY (den Dulk Christian Foundation, 1969) p.iii.

6. Cornelius Van Til A CHRISTIAN THEORY OF KNOWLEDGE (Phillipsburg, N.J.: Presbyterian and Reformed Publishing Company, 1975) p.13.

7. *Ibid.*, pp.12-13.

8. *Ibid.*, p.15.

9. *Ibid.*, p.163.

10. Cornelius Van Til ESSAYS ON CHRISTIAN EDUCATION (Phillipsburg, N.J.: Presbyterian and Reformed Publishing Company, 1974) p.81.

11. J. H. Merle d'Aubigne THE REFORMATION IN ENGLAND Vol. 1, pp.104-105.

12. Jay Adams BACK TO THE BLACKBOARD, p.65.

13. Richard Niebuhr CHRIST AND CULTURE, pp.8-9.

14. Jay Adams BACK TO THE BLACKBOARD, p.65.

15. Cornelius Van Til ESSAYS ON CHRISTIAN EDUCATION, p.203.

16. Robert L. Simonds *National Association of Christian Educators Brochure* (Costa Mesa, CA: NACE).

17. J Gresham Machen CHRISTIANITY AND LIBERALISM (Grand Rapids, MI: Wm. B. Eerdmans Publishing Company, 1983) pp.93-94.

18. Cornelius Van Til DEFENSE OF THE FAITH (Philadelphia, PA: Presbyterian and Reformed Publishing Company, 1976) p.108.

19. Frank E. Gaebelein THE PATTERN OF GOD'S TRUTH: PROBLEMS OF INTEGRATION IN CHRISTIAN EDUCATION (Chicago: Moody Press, 1968) pp.28-29.

20. A. A. Baker THE SUCCESSFUL CHRISTIAN SCHOOL: FOUNDATIONAL PRINCIPLES FOR STARTING AND OPERATING A SUCCESSFUL CHRISTIAN SCHOOL (Pensacola, FL: A Beka Books Publications, 1979) pp.42-49.

21. Cornelius Van Til DEFENSE OF THE FAITH, p.215.

22. Robert J. Eells Creation, Redemption, and Doing Your Best: Gaebelein's Approach to Learning CHRISTIAN APPROACHES TO LEARNING THEORY: A SYMPOSIUM ed. Norma De Jong (Lanbam, MD: University Press, 1984) p.25.

23. Ibid., p.19.

24. Cornelius Van Til A SURVEY OF CHRISTIAN EPISTEMOLOGY, p.123.

25. Abraham Kuyper PRINCIPLES OF SACRED THEOLOGY (Grand Rapids, MI: Baker Book House, 1980) pp.150-154.

26. A. A. Baker THE SUCCESSFUL CHRISTIAN SCHOOL, pp.17-18.

27. J. H. Merle d'Aubigne THE REFORMATION IN ENGLAND, Vol. I, pp.73-74.

28. Cornelius Van Til DEFENSE OF THE FAITH, p.177.

29. Cornelius Van Til ESSAYS ON CHRISTIAN EDUCATION, p.201.

30. Ibid., p.203.

31. Cornelius Van Til A CHRISTIAN THEORY OF KNOWLEDGE, p.297 and THE DEFENSE OF THE FAITH, p.203.

32. Cornelius Van Til CHRISTIAN THEISTIC ETHICS (Nutley, NJ: Presbyterian and Reformed Publishing Company, 1977) p.45.

33. Nicholas Wolterstorff EDUCATING FOR RESPONSIBLE ACTION (Grand Rapids, MI: C.S.I. Publishing, 1980) p.vi.

34. Peter P. DeBoer Toward a Responsibility Theory: Becoming Who We Are, ed., Norman DeJong, CHRISTIAN APPROACHES TO LEARNING: A SYMPOSIUM (Lanham, MD: University Press, 1984) p.122.

35. Jay Adams BACK TO THE BLACKBOARD, pp.86-91, 106-114, 125-130.

36. Geraldine Steensma and Harro W. Van Brummelen, ed., SHAPING SCHOOL CURRICULUM: A BIBLICAL VIEW (Terre Haute, IN: Signal Publishing Corporation, 1977).

37. Cornelius Van Til ESSAYS ON CHRISTIAN EDUCATION, p.191.

38. *Ibid.*

39. Nicholas Wolterstorff EDUCATING FOR RESPONSIBLE ACTION, pp.13-14.

40. Louis Berkhoff *The Covenant of Grace and Its Significance for Christian Education,* FUNDAMENTALS OF CHRISTIAN EDUCATION: THEORY AND PRACTICE, ed. C. Jaarsma (Grand Rapids, MI: Eerdmans Publishing Company, 1953) pp.32-34.

41. *Ibid.,* p.34.

42. *Ibid.,* p.35.

43. Cornelius Van Til ESSAYS ON CHRISTIAN EDUCATION, p.28.

44. A. A. Baker THE SUCCESSFUL CHRISTIAN SCHOOL, pp.30,42.

45. Steensma and Van Brummelen, ed., SHAPING SCHOOL CURRICULUM, p.9.

46. David L. Hocking *The Theological Basis for the Philosophy of Christian School Education,* Paul Krenel, ed., THE PHILOSOPHY OF CHRISTIAN SCHOOL EDUCATION (El Cajon, CA: Christian Heritage College, 1971) p.12-27.

47. Nicholas Wolterstorff EDUCATING FOR RESPONSIBLE ACTION, p.14.

48. Kenneth O. Gangel and Warren S. Benson CHRISTIAN EDUCATION: ITS HISTORY AND PHILOSOPHY (Chicago: Moody Press, 1983) p.343.

49. Cornelius Van Til ESSAYS ON CHRISTIAN EDUCATION, p.124.

50. Roland Bantin HERE I STAND (New York: Abingdon-Cokesbury, nd) p.225.

51. Jay Adams BACK TO THE BLACKBOARD, p.87.

52. J. H. Merle d'Aubigne THE REFORMATION IN ENGLAND, Vol. I, pp.159-161.

53. Jay Adams BACK TO THE BLACKBOARD, p.65.

54. Abraham Kuyper THE WORK OF THE HOLY SPIRIT, trans. Henri De Vries (Grand Rapids MI: Eerdman's Publishing Company, 1946) p.8.

55. *Ibid.,* pp.100-101.

56. *Ibid.,* p.19.

57. *Ibid.,* p.21.

58. Cornelius Van Til *Nature and Scripture,* THE INFALLIBLE WORD: A SYMPOSIUM, eds. N. B. Stonehouse and Paul Woolley (Phillipsburg, NJ: Presbyterian and Reformed Publishing Company, 1980) p.267.

59. Abraham Kuyper THE WORK OF THE HOLY SPIRIT, p.108.

60. *Ibid.,* p.117.

61. *Ibid.,* p.119.

62. Herman Bavinck OUR REASONABLE FAITH, trans. Henry Zylstra (Grand Rapids, MI: Baker Book House, 1977) p.431.

63. Edward J. Carnell AN INTRODUCTION TO CHRISTIAN APOLOGETICS (Grand Rapids, MI: Eerdman's Publishing Company, 1948) p.114.

64. Herman Bavinck OUR REASONABLE FAITH, p.431.

65. John Calvin INSTITUTES OF THE CHRISTIAN RELIGION, Vol. I, ed. John T. McNeill (Philadelphia, PA: The Westminster Press) pp.284-285.

66. *Ibid.,* p.285.

67. *Ibid.,* p.285.

68. J. H. Merle d'Aubigne THE REFORMATION IN ENGLAND, Vol. I and II.

69. Herman Bavinck OUR REASONABLE FAITH, p.415.

70. Abraham Kuyper THE WORK OF THE HOLY SPIRIT, p.492.

PART III
A Biblical School - Theory and Practice

Biblical Christian schools must be built upon God's covenant and must incorporate all the basic considerations discussed in Part II. Upon this foundation, a truly biblical Christian school can be constructed with teachers, students, curriculum and buildings as part of a practicing Christian community. The theoretical structures that have been discussed are absolutely directive for biblical pedagogy. Now we must proceed to develop an actual Christian educational system. We can not remain speculative or abstract, but together, we must transform biblical principles of education and learning into actual Christian schools with genuine biblical curriculum.

This is a significant step. It is a step that the Puritans failed to take.

> There is no denying that the Puritans had a zeal for learning . . . [but] they never produced anything like a logical Puritan curriculum. They glorified the Bible, but never worked out a course of study for which the one book would be the basis. The chief end was to glorify God, but Puritan students spent most of their time reading heathen authors. . . . [D]efinite religious instruction was largely a weekend affair, and the Bible was not commonly used as a school text. . . . There is nowhere to be found the genuine Christian curriculum which readers of popular expositions of Calvin's "thoroughgoing logic" might be led to expect.[1]

Christian educators in the Twentieth Century are beginning to take this vital step. Genuine biblical curriculum is being developed. Previously, Christian curriculum was limited to Bible-class studies, a limited synthesis of Bible verses and factual content, tight classroom rules, and some adherence to the ten commandments. Take, for example, the experience of one of my former high school students. I had encouraged her to go to a Christian college. She had a good idea of what it meant to think, study and learn from a Christian perspective. In her freshman biology class, the professor started out with a list of Bible verses which pertained to biology. After a brief discussion, he said,

"Now, back to biology." This student dropped out of Christian college. She may not have known what genuine biblical curriculum would be if she ever experienced it, but she certainly knew that it was not a part of this so-called Christian science course.

Unfortunately, the lack of a truly biblical curriculum is still a major problem. Many Christian publishers, writers and educators are attempting to correct this problem. We believe that most of these efforts are shallow, restricting and fall far short of the scope of what biblical curriculum ought to be for God's covenant children. Therefore, the following is presented as a brief introduction to a fresh and distinctively biblical view of curriculum which is in actual practice. Please consider the ideas with constructive criticism and share your suggestions, ideas, questions and improvements with us.

Introducing Ministry-Learning for Christian Schools

It is our purpose in Part III to introduce you to the concept of Ministry-Learning for biblical Christian schools. We intend to briefly discuss this concept by contrasting it to "traditional Christian education" and "progressive Christian education." The biblical principles discussed in Parts I and II should be recalled while reading this section. Then, building upon the distinctives of Ministry-Learning, we unfold various aspects of our view. First, a short review of current writers who have pioneered this approach is presented, followed by an overview of our approach, which we call Ministry-Learning for Christian schools. Second, eight key elements or components of Ministry-Learning are discussed. These components are designed to give you a basic understanding of how Ministry-Learning works in actual Christian schools. Ministry-Learning is not simply an abstract ideal. There are Christian schools where these ideas are being successfully practiced.

Many Christian school leaders talk about various kinds of Christian schools. Most Christian schools are traditional and are fearful of progressive education. "Traditional Christian education," according to Baker, "is teaching individuals language (effective reading, writing, and speaking according to the conventions of their culture and the universal laws of logic) and subject matter (Bible, history, literature, science, mathematics, music, art). It is also the training of character through rules, principles and formation of habit."[2] In other words, traditionalists believe that there is a given body of knowledge which every student must acquire, thus, "the curriculum must be truth-centered."[3] John Dewey describes traditional education as follows:

> The subject matter of education consists of bodies of information and skills that have been worked out in the past [including, for Christians, the Bible]; therefore, the chief business of the school is to transmit them to the new generation. . . . The main purpose or objective is to prepare the young for future responsibilities and success in life, by means of acquisition of the organized bodies of information and prepared forms of skill which comprehend the material of instruction. . . . The traditional scheme is, in essence, one of imposition from above and from outside.[4]

Traditional Christian education seems to be comprised of a body of information which must be deposited in the mind-banks of students.

On the other hand, Christian progressive education emphasizes "the unity of the person, the education of the whole man, and the primacy of love."[5] This latter approach is student-centered in its implementation of curriculum. Progressive education in Dewey's model includes: cultivation of individuality, free activity, learning through experience, acquisition of isolated skills and techniques as a means of attaining ends which make direct and vital appeal, making the most of the opportunities of the present, and acquaintance with a changing world. "There is an intimate and necessary relation between the process of actual experience and education,"[6] claims Dewey. Parents ordinarily associate unlimited student freedom with this view; students learning when and what they want, little or no teacher authority, a total lack of discipline, and Dewey's atheistic beliefs.

Christian traditional education is popular with fundamentalist and evangelical Christian schools. Schools with a reformed emphasis tend to have elements of both traditional and progressive education. In both cases, basics are emphasized and, to some degree, all of these schools attempt to teach students by meeting their physical, mental, emotional and spiritual needs.

Secular private schools and public schools are also traditional or progressive in their approach to education. They do not attempt to be spiritual educators but do believe that they are teaching traditional values and true facts, and that they are educating the whole student by allowing for freedom of religion. It seems that most Christian school educators, traditional or progressive, attempt to *integrate* Christian values and facts into the teaching-learning process and, thereby, are also spiritual educators. Using the Bible, these educators believe that they can integrate this "missing ingredient" into the curriculum, classroom lesson or school administration and, thus, construct a viable Christian school with valid Christian learning.

Strong criticism has been directed at both traditional and progressive education, Christian and non-Christian. Peter F. Drucker, a progressivist, has written that there are tremendous differences in rhythm, attention span and learning pace, especially among young children. If they are suppressed, as all traditional schooling has to do, "dumb children are created. If they are used, however, learning energies are liberated."[7] He is not suprised that students are bored stiff by school and that the classroom is despised for being irrelevant. Daryl Borgquist, from the United States Department of Education, is critical of traditional education when he notes that centralized control of curriculum takes away liberty.[8] Hence, there is a call for a decentralized curriculum. Educators and parents, in particular, are beginning to realize that their schools have come under alien control. Organizations like the National Education Association or publishers like A Beka Books, or Accelerated Christian Education have successfully taken control of thousands of schools by centralizing curriculum. They control what facts are taught, the interpretation of the facts, the amount of time spent on subject matter, the means and method of student evaluation, teacher work load, teaching methods, teacher in-service meetings, school budgets and a host of other areas of schooling. Textbook publishers know that 50 percent of the students educated by public schools live in nine states. Accordingly, their textbooks are written to maximize sales in this limited market. What controls curriculum content is material that will sell in these areas, not specific student needs or relevancy. Biblical liberty for Christian teachers and students, to learn and to actively carry out the special calling that God has specifically planned for each covenant student, cannot be adequately achieved while under foreign control wielded by powerful teacher organizations or curriculum publishers.

Although we do not affirm Dewey's philosophy of education, he does point out numerous flaws in traditional education. He notes that the impetus to learn is lost due to boring processes. The skills acquired by automatic drill impair the power of judgment and capacity to act intelligently in new situations. Learning in the classroom is foreign to real life situations which are outside the school. Traditional education pays little attention to the internal factors of each student or, due to external control, the internalization of factual interpretation and values remains undetermined. It fails to adapt educational materials and curriculum to the needs and capacities of individuals by imposing artificial uniformity. Despite Dewey's non-Christian position, we should note that these defects are important to Christian educators because many of them point out the non-Christian nature of traditional education. Covenant students ought not be bored with learning God's thoughts after God, and Christian educators cannot fail to adapt to the individual capacities that God has given to each student under their care.

In contrast to the Christian traditionalist position, Christian progressivists emphasize the scientific and psychological aspects of child and student development. They attempt to use some of the scientific observations of John Dewey, Jean Piaget and others, but also retain the theology and philosophy of Herman Bavinck. In other instances, psychological concepts are integrated with subject matter or truth, and it is claimed that this produces Christian learning. The students' perceived needs, based on empirical science, are met and truth is biblically understood through the integration of science and the Bible; therefore, it is believed that each covenant student is being formed into what God created him to be. Moreover, of primary importance is the need for redemption as it is true that "Covenant youth, too, must be converted."[9] To be sure, redemption is essential but it is not in itself Christian education. It is the starting point for Christian education. Regeneration is the foundation that Christian progressivists attempt to use to catapult students from spiritual looking activities to genuine Christian cultural activities which in turn transforms them into servants of God.

Christian progressivists were criticized for being anti-intellectual because they seemed to dilute learning content and neglect basic skills, for compromising biblical theology and philosophy with science and psychology, for being too child-centered in their view of freedom, and for an over-emphasis on redemption which is not balanced by appropriate covenantal possession of the creational and cultural spheres.

Nicholas Wolterstorff has led Christians in constructing a new Christian learning theory. He has been critical of the other two views. "[Christian] education," he insisted, "must not be a passive, absorbent process . . . [Christian]'education should not be like a kettle with water. It should be like lighting a fire under the kettle."[10] Thus, Wolterstorff directed Christian educators away from the blank-slate concept of John Locke which permeates traditional Christian education. An emphasis was placed on student needs, creativity, choice, responsibility, and activity in all of life which must go beyond the incomplete transformation of Christian progressivists.

Our solution to the defects in both Christian traditional and progressive education is the concept of Ministry-Learning. Ministry-Learning is a three-fold work of the Spirit of God. Learning skills and factual content are concretely brought together through ministry projects and learning experiences which are a part of genuine service ministry. Together, all three form the components of Ministry-Learning. Basic learning skills and all factual content are always determined by and interpreted under subjection to the absolute authority of the Bible. These aspects are learned concretely or experienced through the construction of ministry projects or various learning activities. The projects and experiences are not simply plastic models for pretend acts of ministry. Rather, they are foundational to and part of a genuine student ministry. In brief, Ministry-Learning is a learning system where students learn while serving God.

There seem to be some revised elements of Christian traditional and progressive education in our conception of Ministry-Learning. This may appear true because of our emphasis on biblical absolutes and the acquisition of learning skills. We also emphasize meeting individual student needs, biblical freedom and responsibility, learning through concrete learning activities and custom designed curriculum for each student. The similarities we acknowledge but insist that Ministry-Learning, when taken as a whole, is a distinct and biblical system for learning.

Ministry-Learning
A Biblical View of Integral Curriculum

Christian learning theory and practice is beginning to be clarified in circles of Christian educators. Leaders who have made significant contributions include Nicholas Wolterstorff, Geraldine Steensma and Jay Adams. These three deserve brief review.

Wolterstorff

According to Peter De Boer, Wolterstorff has staked out "a middle way, drawing on the best of both Christian traditionalism and Christian progressivism."[11] Wolterstorff believes that understanding is important for the learner, but understanding alone is insufficient. He wanted Christian curriculum to arm covenant learners to live the Christian life - not just to understand it. Therefore, he promotes the notion that a covenant learner is "both a creature of consciousness who must learn 'what is the case' and a creature of action, of 'free, reasonable action."[12] This enabled him to plot out five standards for Christian curriculum. These standards - the life of man, the life of faith, the life of someone who is a member of the Christian community, the life to be lived in the midst of ordinary human society, and the life engaged in helping to carry out man's task of cultural dominion[13] - brought into focus essential components of biblical Christian education. They emphasized the wholeness of man, active service, the uniqueness of each student, responsible action, covenant community, Christ transforming culture, and creative thinking and speaking.

Steensma

The work of Steensma goes beyond Wolterstorff because she has not only constructed Christian curriculum theory but has actually put her insights into practice. She believes that there is a "constant struggle in deciding when and how much to emphasize conceptual learning yet provide experiences that promote loving service in the name of Christ."[14] Steensma believes that the skills and content of Christian curriculum must incite a multitude of actions. Skills and content, without action, are alien to the real world God created, and they do not fit with what it means to have "knowledge" in the Old Testament sense or "knowing" in the New Testament concept of the word. On the other hand, action which is faithful to the biblical concept of truth, must be organically rooted with biblical understanding of content and skills if the action is to have eternal significance and stand in contrast to non-Christian humanitarian action.

For Steensma, the biblical concept of truth means "loving in deed, not only in word" (John 3:18).[15] In other words, students are to "acquire all the information of which they are capable. However, their information may not stand in isolation from a call to service." Therefore, "without compromising service to God," student-learning includes action, loving deeds, a developing Christian lifestyle, service to society, and creative-cultural growth which flower from the bud of biblically understood skills and content.[16]

Adams

Christian education, according to Adams, is made clear by the biblical word, *wisdom*. In the Bible, the word, *wisdom*, brings together three factors: knowledge, life and ministry. It is knowledge understood from God's perspective, made profitable for day-to-day living for Him, and (as part of that) shared with others and used to minister to them."[17] Adams advocates that "Truth is for use . . . and is taught in the Bible by the phrase, "walking in the truth." Therefore, "every fact that [the Christian student] acquires must be (1) oriented properly into his Christian life, placing God's interpretation on it, and (2) turned into life and ministry."[18]

Ministering projects is the program set forth by Adams. He believes that teachers should guide Christian students in choosing ministering projects which are "genuine tasks in which actual ministry is carried on."[19] Adams believes that the school campus is the entire community.[20] For example, a project might be grocery shopping for a shut-in senior citizen. In order to achieve this ministering service, the students involved will keep this God-glorifying goal in the front of their minds while they learn the necessary reading, mathematic, social and economic skills and/or factual content which are necessary to implement the task. Adams believes that this approach emphasizes God-given individualization, Spirit-directed motivation, and skills or curriculum content. Creative thinking and talent or gift usage are enhanced. The proper relationship between the home and school is cultivated and biblical discipleship is fostered by this program of life and ministry.

Maffet-McMillan

Our approach to Christian education is to build on Wolterstorff, Steensma and Adams. We stand firmly upon the historical and reformed creeds in order to develop our educational ideology and our practice at Grace Christian School.

In brief, our educational design is a three-stage process, illustrated below. The numbered arrows indicate the cycle which our teaching-learning design is to follow, and they establish the relationship between each stage.

Three—Stage Ministry—Learning Curriculum Process

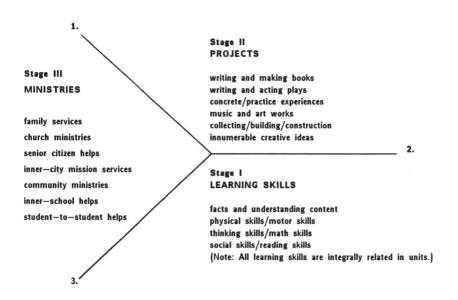

1.

Stage II
PROJECTS

Stage III
MINISTRIES

writing and making books
writing and acting plays
concrete/practice experiences
music and art works

family services
church ministries
collecting/building/construction
innumerable creative ideas

senior citizen helps
2.

inner—city mission services
Stage I

community ministries
LEARNING SKILLS

inner—school helps
facts and understanding content

student—to—student helps
physical skills/motor skills
thinking skills/math skills
social skills/reading skills
(Note: All learning skills are integrally related in units.)

3.

Our method begins by setting before the students an actual, true-to-life ministry that the students can do for the glory of God (Stage III). In order to carry out a specific ministry, specific tools will be needed (Stages I and II). These tools come in the form of projects developed by the students, and in the specific learning skills and factual content required to develop the projects and ministry tasks. In this way, both learning skills, factual content and project experiences are relevant to real life because they are to be *used to minister* for the glory of God. We have called this Ministry-Learning.

The learning of skills and factual content have traditionally been the principal focus of educators. Usually the skills are divided into abstract subject areas like reading, spelling, arithmetic, science and history. In our model, skills are held in balance with projects and ministry services. Notwithstanding, there is a strong emphasis on learning skills and factual content. The skills in Stage I do not stand in isolation. God's creation cannot be understood without acknowledging this fundamental interrelatedness. Creation, and thus, all of education, "is like a beautiful tapestry." The threads of mathematics, art, history, science, and literature are woven together. "The true understanding of any one of them is distorted if you pluck that thread from the weaving."[21] Moreover, the tapestry project is to be actually used for specific Christian ministry.

Integral curriculum is designed to uphold the interrelatedness of God's creation. Rather than promote a fragmented curriculum of diverse learning skills and factual content, we teach the academic subjects, simultaneously, in units. For example, a unit on "Insects" may be introduced to the students. During the time the unit is being studied, the students read about insects, draw them, research what the Bible says about them, spell insect-related words, study what biblically directed scientific experimentation has revealed about insect life, identify how God uses insects, and catch, touch, raise, dissect and collect them. Our students experience these creatures in a biblical relationship. Thus, subject areas are kept in their context of meaning as God created them for everyday life. There are numerous skills and facts associated with the various subjects or dimensions of creation and "each dimension influences and affects every other dimension."[22] In other words, "all of creation is *integrated* because that's the way God made it; therefore, that's the way we experience it. People do not *make* an integral, coherent world; the creation is integral [or integrated] in its very being. . . ."[23]

At Grace Christian School, the teacher introduces a unit theme to the students. A unit may be titled *Plants, Insects, Water,* or *The Human Body*. Each unit is studied in all of its dimensions with the appropriate learning skills coordinated with the student's ability level and interest. Dimensions of creation are numeral, spatial, biological, emotional, historical, lingual, social, economic, aesthetic, legal, confessional and moral.[24] The unit is studied by each student in all of its dimensions and in accord with the skills and facts associated with them. So, skills and facts are studied in the coherent relationship in which God created them, and they have immediate meaning for life since the student understands them as part of a unit with projects and ministry activity.

An excellent example of integral, educational relationship is provided by Al Green.[25] Notice how all the traditional subject areas flow from a single unit or topic area.

Unit	Facts/Content Area	Subject Area
	baptism	confessional [Bible, theology]
	purity vs. pollution	moral [values]
	fishing rights	legal [government, law]
	thing of beauty	aesthetic [art, interior design]
	water bill	economic [economics, finance]
	common cup	social [urban studies, sociology]
GLASS	babbling brook	language [literature, grammar, writing]
OF	Red Sea	historical [U.S. history, world history]
WATER	emotional "high"	emotional [psychology]
	analytical chemistry	analytical [logic, thinking skills]
	thirst quencher	biological [biology, botany]
	H_2O	physical [chemistry]
	water power	motion [physics]
	block of ice	spatial [architecture, geometry]
	one glass	numeral [mathematics]

The above illustration sets forth the integral relationship between all the aspects of God's creation. A unit titled, *A Glass of Water*, incorporates all the dimensions of creation and thus represents all the subject areas. Green is using the unit to teach specifics about any given dimension while also teaching the specifics in the relationship God has established with all the other dimensions. A glass of water never stands in isolation from the dimensions of creation. It is integrally related to all the dimensions because that is the way God made the world to operate. We must teach our students about the content in every dimension and about the relationship God established between the content and all the other dimensions. We call this integral curriculum because all the dimensions of creation are taught in an integral relationship. In addition, Green points out that units of study are prepared from the main divisions of subject matter: man as an individual person, mankind in a social group, animals, plants, and earth or space. The *Glass of Water* unit is from the earth or space division of subject matter.

The Biblical School in Practice

There are several key practices which are vital for Christian teaching and curriculum to be truly biblical. We have listed eight areas of practice which are central to implementing Ministry-Learning in concert with the biblical view of integral curriculum. These practices are simply a beginning and make no claim to be exhaustive. They are designed to set forth some initial steps toward putting Ministry-Learning into use by Christian school educators. The biblical view of integral curriculum is the route we suggest. We believe that this route is most consistent with our covenant foundation and Christian philosophy of education, set forth in Parts I and II.

a. Christian Curriculum, Learning and Design

Biblical curriculum, learning and design are aimed at nurturing students to actively build a Christian world-order. As Christian people living under biblical directives, we seek to educate God's covenant children according to God's plan for them and His design for creation. The dominion arrangement of the Christian world-order is subject to the biblical rule and law of God and this includes the subjection of our curriculum, learning and design. Teachers and students are to biblically rule over curriculum, learning and design, and not be ruled by them. Accordingly, the Christian school must work out a view of curriculum, learning and design which is in keeping with the biblical Christian world-order.

Christian educators use curriculum to equip and provide actual, ministry experiences for students. Curriculum is used to proclaim commitment to Christ and to reveal God's claim on *all* of one's life. "It is to this end that the curriculum must be used to guide students in discerning the faith commitment at the root of what they are studying."[26] This is far more than acquiring information. Our view of curriculum will prepare students for a life in God's service by using their talents, skills and information for service to God in the present. Students learn and understand that their lives are to be rooted wholly in Christ and they learn how to intimately associate information, understanding and a life of Christian service with a full-orbed biblical faith commitment. In brief, this is Ministry-Learning.

Curriculum at biblical Christian schools must be developed to take into account how individual students interact with God and the varying forms of God's creation: things, plants, animals and other men. This interaction changes as students grow and mature through the different levels of mental, physical, emotional and spiritual development. The multiform biblical relationships which each student has with God, his fellowman and creation must unfold throughout the school curriculum and be directive of curriculum. All too often it is curriculum that has directive dominion, authority or rule over students. This is contrary to Genesis 1:26,27, where God says that man is to have dominion. If a student is biblically God-conscious then his growth will be readily noted in obedient living, academic achievement, and dominion ministry. Christian school ministry must be determined, in part, by this God-consciousness. On the other hand, when a student is suppressing biblical God-consciousness, then the curriculum must be changed to combat disobedient living, academic decay and ego-service.

Interaction with the various forms of creation and with God will develop for Christian students a curriculum unity. Students will begin to comprehend and experience a God-given unity of knowledge and life. No longer is curriculum to be fragmented into subjects, courses or disciplines. For example, history and science are studied in their biblical relationship. A *historical* study of Christopher Columbus sailing west, across the Atlantic Ocean in 1492, to discover a new route to China, is greatly enhanced if the students also study the *science* of Fifteenth Century sailing. This is called *integral education.* Nonetheless, science, history or any subject may be abstractly separated from its world context for particular fact-finding, but they must readily be comprehended, interpreted or understood in the integral relationship of God's creation relationship. The distinction between fact-finding and integral education is essential for Christian learning and living. They are in a supplementary and reciprocal relationship.

The area of moral or values education is of special interest to educators and parents, and it provides a good illustration of the supplementary and reciprocal relationship between fact-finding and integral education. Often Christians and non-Christians view some acts as moral and others as amoral. In other words, at times the concept of right and wrong has something to do with human actions while at other times right and wrong seem to have nothing to do with other human actions. We believe that *all* human actions, learning and thinking are morally right or morally wrong. The moral aspect or sphere is intimately united with the biblical understanding of every fact and every action. There is no moral neutrality. Morality is a vital and continuous part of every man's relationship with God or God's creation. All human thought and action starts in moral righteousness with God or are condemned in moral unrighteousness. There are no exceptions. Our Christian school curriculum must set forth this moral relationship and develop it as a vital part of all other relationships. So it is, also, with the relationships among spelling, grammar, reading, mathematics, and all other subjects. They must all be taught in their integral relationship.

"Learning is meaningful only if the wholeness of life and the unity of creation becomes clear to the student."[27] A fact learned, a skill acquired or a subject taught becomes meaningful to the student when it is comprehended and acted upon in relationship to all the spheres of creation. Specifically, this is true when it is tied directly to each student's real-life context. Included at the outset of meaningful learning for Christian students is their faith-commitment to the God of the Bible. All other views about ·learning have a false faith commitment at the outset, and thus, can never become ultimately meaningful; nor can they conclude with wholeness of life and unity of knowledge. Biblical curriculum must set forth the truth that "God is before all things, and in Him all things hold together" (Col 1:17 N.I.V.). To depart from this unity is to isolate the thinking of the mind from the actual world in which we live. Isolated thinking, drill and practice must be brought into focus by the student comprehending them as part of all the created spheres and as part of their genuine service for the Lord. Simply teaching facts or skills is not true biblical education.

An example of meaningful learning could be the skill of writing a letter. Letter writing skills can easily be taught as part of any unit because students can use them to acquire information or to acknowledge assistance given on every theme or topic. Then, too, even within the isolated letter writing activity, as this example shows, the skills are clearly integral in their relationship with all areas of God's creation. If a student was able to write a letter with the appropriate form, it would be a meaningless exercise if there were no use for letters in our culture. On the contrary, the acquisition of letter writing skills becomes a meaningful learning experience when the student comprehends that we have a mail service, that letters are used to conduct business and personal affairs, and that the very letter they write in school is to be used to communicate to others and ultimately to minister for the glory of God. Included in this is an understanding of postal service *economics; history,* because letters are written in one point in time and received in another; *science* is used in the development of paper and ink; and *art work* in the letterhead design. Readily, *ethics, social skills,* and other spheres of creation can be integrally related to the *language art skill* of letter writing. Such integral relationships unify and enhance learning and are ultimately valuable because their relationship to God is clearly seen and practiced in service to Him.

Rosina, a senior citizen who attended a nearby adult day care center, recently died. Our students sent sympathy letters and illustrated cards to her daughter. On several previous occasions, our children had ministered to Rosina and the other senior citizens with songs, crafts, plays, readings and through celebrations. They had enjoyed sharing, giving, serving and ministering to Rosina in a concrete, personal manner. Their ministry was not abstract or futuristic. It used the various skills taught them at their skill levels for actual glorification of God. In response to these cards, we received the following letter.

Dear Children and Teachers,

Your cards of sympathy and wishes for my good health were such a joy to me. I will keep them forever. I have a friend who is an art teacher. I want to show them to her. I thought they were excellent. Some of you are future artists and all of you are a product of our Lord's great work!

Your teachers are special, too. They are teaching you what the best things are.

God Bless All of You,

Since every student's learning situation or context is different, their approach to learning will differ. Biblical Christian teachers design curriculum to take this into account. Every student is different. They view the various aspects of creation differently; they arrange facts in their minds in different relationships or contexts; they build or construct concepts differently; they see things in different order and with various emphasis. Suppose we ask two boys to describe a dog. One boy describes a big, black, short-haired Doberman with pointed ears, sharp teeth and a chain collar, while the other boy describes a little, brown and white mutt which runs free to play with him. Both boys have correctly described a dog, but due to their unique experiences and learning situations, their conceptualization of a dog differs. Students reveal different fears, sensitivites, perceptions and opinion values. Since God has ordained that each student's learning situation is different, so must be their curriculum.

Learning advances when students comprehend new facts or skills within the biblical conception of God's world which includes their ministry activities. Steensma notes that this is accomplished in two ways. First, primary students "appear to be romancing or playing with reality."[28] When they explore new things, the teacher may ask "Why?" or "What if?" questions in order to guide them to establish relationships, form opinions and develop conclusions. They have fun learning while touching and sensing things, enjoying field trips, and actively using them to delight in God and glorify Him. Students are learning while physically experiencing the unity of creation in an unstructured learning environment. This is called inductive thinking. Second, students need to organize their conception of God's world. They must go beyond romancing and begin to clarify their learning with precision instruction, logical order, practice, drill and organization, all in accord with biblical teaching principles. This involves rational thinking and may be called deductive thinking.

The advancement of learning involves both romance and precision. There is fun with exploration and there is organized work with precision instruction. For example, when a student is learning to write, he might have fun making all kinds of lines and circles on a blank paper. He is playing with the pencil and enjoying the discovery of various forms he can create through unorganized thought. Then the teacher provides precise instruction on how to write the letters of the alphabet. The student must now work by practicing, ordering and organizing his thoughts. Both types of thinking activities are necessary for student learning.

Christian traditional educators tend to focus on organized work while Christian progressive educators tend to focus on romancing exploration. In contrast to those views, Christian educators using the biblical view of integral-learning understand the essential relationship of both organized work and romancing exploration, and then go beyond them both into project development and actual ministry-learning. Traditionalists often create boring, tiresome, dull and repetitive learning situations, while progressivists create an overabundance of opportunity for students to pursue selfish passions. In opposition to both Christian traditionalists and progressivists, the Christian integralists place before the student, from the outset, the purpose and place of both romancing and organized work activities. Students know before a new learning situation is presented by the teacher that a specific service ministry is to be performed by using their new learning. Students, therefore are to responsibly and voluntarily commit their learning activities to actualized ministry which relieves boredom and irresponsibility because the focus is serving God.

Christian curriculum and learning must begin with and be designed upon the Bible. The Bible must serve as the foundation for curriculum and learning and it must be used to actively direct them. Steensma and Van Brummelen have suggested a biblically based and biblically directed design for Christian school curriculum.[29] Some key points from their curriculum design are as follows:

1. Curriculum design is grounded and directed by the Bible.

2. Skill development is essential and must be integrally related to all spheres of God's creation; not held in isolation but intimately associated with the content of all aspects of reality and with actual Christian service.

3. At the elementary level, the skill areas flow from and back into the content areas of God's unified creation.

4. At the secondary level, the unity of creation must be maintained with a core program which relates all specialty curriculum areas with the biblical focus of a Christian world-order.

5. Project work and Christian service should be actively practiced in the local community. During the primary years most of this activity will center within the containment of the home, school and church but, as the students mature, their community outreach begins to embrace all social spheres; government services, community agencies, mass media, social work, legal and medical services, and all other labor forces.

The above curriculum design points are illustrated in the diagram below. In addition, earlier curriculum and learning points are incorporated as an example.

Certainly much work remains in this area of curriculum development. The major changes that are needed in our high schools require much time and effort to accomplish. No longer do we tolerate teachers lecturing verbatim from textbooks, then quizzing, and finally testing students on thoroughly stale material. It will not do for our high school students to simply memorize the content from a half-dozen courses, a content poured out in 45 minute spoon-fed lots each day. A bridge over the chasm between subject areas must be made. The fragmentation between subjects is not conducive to thinking, "as on any given day a student needs to remember a hodgepodge of chemistry and cooking, literature and math, French and biology."[30]

It's time to get our change oriented talk into action. We are attempting to point the way, to proceed as the Spirit enables and to encourage others. Our ideas will need to be tested, revised, refined and restated.

FLOWCHART — PRIMARY DEVELOPMENTAL YEARS

STEP 1

Begin with the biblical faith commitment

STEP 2 *

Students explore the world around them

Skills are acquired with the aid of precision instruction

STEP 3 **

Primary projects and ministry service tasks

in the home/school church

* Integrally related units for skill and factual content learning using inductive and deductive experiences.

** These three steps form a unified field of knowledge which is representative of a unified creation.

FLOWCHART — SECONDARY DEVELOPMENTAL YEARS

STEP 1

Begin with the biblical faith commitment

STEP 2

Core curriculum area — all subjects are integrally unified

with generalized skills and facts

Specialty curriculum areas designed for extraordinary

skills/talents/interests/content using both

exploration and precision instruction.

STEP 3

Secondary projects and ministry service tasks

originate from the biblical faith commitment

and are praticed in both core and specialty

curriculum areas. Together they form a

unified field of knowledge, which is

representative of a unified creation, and

actively implemented in all community

spheres of society.

---

b. Textbooks and Curriculum Materials

One of the first questions asked by educators who are being introduced to Ministry-Learning, particularly to the biblical view of integral curriculum is, "What books do you use?" In rapid fire, they want to know publishers names and addresses, if teachers guides are available, what the costs are, if the workbooks may be copied, and the rationale for a particular textbook series.

Our reaction to this is to de-emphasize textbooks. We desire to reduce and eliminate textbook dependency. The Bible is the only indispensable book, yet, it seems as if teachers need other textbooks in order to teach. In fact, it is true that many teachers teach by simply unpacking the contents of textbooks. Without textbooks, they would be lost and unable to educate; with textbooks, most students could learn without their textbook-dependent teachers.

Textbooks and related curriculum materials are valuable tools. We advocate the use of textbooks, but we do not believe that textbooks should determine the curriculum. Biblical curriculum is determined by a host of factors: biblical law, student abilities and interests, relevancy to God's world, the Spirit's direction, specific ministry tasks, the dominion mandate, covenant responsibilities, and the unique blessings God gives to each person. Textbooks are to be used in subserviency to these curriculum factors.

To answer the question, "What textbooks do you use?" we state that a large variety of texts from numerous publishers, both Christian and non-Christian, are used. Christian publishers may produce some good books but many of their products are not based upon a biblical view of teaching or learning, often fail to interpret facts biblically, and frequently define words or concepts apart from God's denotation.

We suggest that classrooms be supplied with a few textbooks from each publisher rather than a large quantity of the same text from a single publisher. For example, if we want to purchase history texts, we may buy three texts from seven different publishers. This would give us access to twenty-one books containing seven different accounts of historical events. Students, by sharing, would have the opportunity to read several views of history. If they were studying a unit on American inventors, it would be valuable for them to comprehend the topic from different vantage points, and to compare and contrast them to God's perspective while integrating their learning in a specific ministry project.

Often standard textbooks would not be needed. To continue our example in history, there is much more information about American inventors assembled in books which are specifically written on the topic than in general history textbooks. Teachers and students could go to the library and check out thirty different books which contain biographic, scientific, economic, legal and environmental information about noted inventors and their inventions. Again, by exchanging books, students have greater opportunity to acquire more learning content than in classes taught by textbook-dependent teachers and, in this case, students can readily comprehend the integral relationship between subject areas or spheres of reality.

There are many other strategies which can be used to enhance student learning and break away from textbooks. Look at the following:

1. New spelling words can be obtained by students from their pleasure reading books or magazines. They can create and keep their own spelling word lists. My son can identify hundreds of new spelling words from reading his fishing magazines. They are words he wants to know - relevant to his interests. By practicing individual curriculum management, the teacher can guide him to use these words in a ministry project.

2. Students studying correct grammar may practice identifying verbs or prepositional phrases by working from their own writing projects or the writings of other students. These skills can be taught using library books. Students may minister to each other by writing sentences and exchanging them to exercise their skills. In this way, they learn in a real life context rather than doing drill exercises which are abstract from their personal lives or reality.

3. Elementary reading comprehension skills do not have to be acquired by students reading their textbook readers and answering the same questions prescribed for thousands of students. Some students are able to choose a children's story book as a reader. At the end of each chapter or after completing the book, students may orally retell the story to other students, construct puppets to act out the story, or rewrite the story in their own words. This approach allows students to read books that are relevant to the unit they are studying or that are of special interest. Students may be using a variety of learning

methods to acquire the skills, and they may use the skills to minister to others. Different books, learning methods, and ministries are unfolding for each student while they all develop their reading comprehension skills.

c. Skill Achievement Records

Student evaluation is of primary interest to educators, parents and students. The traditional grading system, with its A's, B's and F's, seems to be universally accepted by both Christians and non-Christians. The progressive non-graded system has been rejected by most educators. However, as Christians, we must be certain that our evaluation system is biblical.

Is the traditional grading system biblical? A resounding "No!" is our reply. Adams has pointed out several biblical reasons why traditional grades are unacceptable.[31] Some of the reasons are as follows:

1. God has given all Christians various gifts. Each student has different gifts and they are to be used in different kinds of ministry. At times God gives the same gift in different measures for different purposes. How can Christians validly grade students without also grading God's gift giving or the Holy Spirit's use of the gifts?

2. The Bible teaches that students should be motivated to use their God-given gifts because it is their covenant responsibility to please God. Students are to be motivated by the Holy Spirit to become the best persons God intends in order that they may serve Him to the fullest extent of their abilities. However, in the traditional grading system, grades become an idol. Students are encouraged to worship grades because good grades please parents, enable them to enter college, and win praise from teachers and peers.

3. The Bible does not teach that academic gifts should be lifted above non-academic gifts. All the gifts God gives are perfect. Educators are judging God when they grade academic gifts, just as they would be judging God for His appropriation of the gifts of the Spirit - love, joy, peace. By emphasizing "high academic standards," Christian prep schools fail to rightly lift up *all* of

God's gifts and tend to belittle students who are not gifted with extra academic competence.

4. Grades are immoral because they are reportedly *objective* and because they supposedly record an individual's achievements. They are said to be the "marks" which have been "earned" through "testing." These claims are a lie. Grades are subjective and do not measure only the work of an individual student. Rather, grades are based on teacher opinion, the teacher's choice of words and questions, and the subjective feelings, emotions or moods of both teachers and students. Grades may tell more about the teacher and school than they do about an individual student. Paul Springstubb points out that "grading ... does little to encourage thinking. ... An intellectual give-and-take among students does not lend itself to point tallies; a student's thoughtful opinion can hardly be graded B- or C+. ... [Grades] can lead to interminable quizzes, points for this and points for that, hundreds upon hundreds of points, all of which are utterly irrelevant to whether or not that student has spent a solitary moment thinking about the meaning of what he has studied."[32]

Other reasons that grades are a poor system for evaluation include: they promote cheating; they support bad teaching; they foster unbiblical student competition; they encourage false pride; and they destroy the proper ego of less academically gifted students.

Horror stories can be told about grades. Consider Jennifer. She correctly answered 29 of 30 questions on her Bible test. A grade of "F" was given because she neglected to write her name on her paper. How does this rightly evaluate her Bible knowledge?

Grades in physical education are also a farce. Students blessed by God with superior speed, coordination and motor skill routinely are given the grade of A. Students with average physical abilities are given lower grades which often depend on their weight, and statistical norms for strength and speed. Sometimes physical education grades depend on how often students wear their P.E. uniforms, or if they shower after class. This is not biblical evaluation.

As a young man of fourteen years, I was "tested" at the Reading Clinic, in the Department of Psychology at Temple University. The tests concluded that I was "not seriously retarded." Perhaps if this information was known to me at an earlier date, I would never have attempted the doctorate program at Akron University. Certainly, I thank God that He rules in my life, not the grades given me by biased teachers and testing programs. Much has been written on this subject. Read THE TYRANNY OF TESTING by Banesh Hoffmann to learn more about the damaging effects of the exaggerated claims of test psychologists.

* * * * *

Instead of grades, we suggest that skill records be kept in portfolios of student work. Like an architect or an artist, a collection of student work is kept to demonstrate abilities and progress. Examples of creative writing, mathematical computations and actual projects which the student has completed are put in the portfolio. Also, video cassettes, audio recordings, letters of recommendation and (if you must) "standardized testing" scores are kept with attendance and health records. Individual student Skill Achievement Records are kept there too.

Skill Achievement Records are of primary importance. An example of this type of record is illustrated below. This sample *Skill Achievement Record* represents but a few of the hundreds of skills recorded and monitored by the teacher. By using these forms, teachers are able to track the skill development of each individual student. According to the student's interests, gifts and environmental context, teachers may plan specific learning-skill activites for every student . A personalized, custom-made curriculum can be developed for every student with the skills providing structure. As skills are achieved, the teacher checks them and, thereby, indicates that the student has mastered them. When parents review the *Skill Achievement Record*, they know exactly what their child can do and what has been accomplished since the previous review. In contrast to this clear communication of student skill achievement, grades like A+ or B- give only glittering generalities and no specific information.

Skills furnish the framework for the teacher to develop each student's personalized curriculum. *These skills are determined by biblical norms for man.* God's biblical commands, principles, laws and expectations are the basis for the skills contained in the *Skill Record.* The skills required to achieve these biblical duties are

---

SKILL ACHIEVEMENT RECORD [33]

AUDITORY DISCRIMINATION   2/86   5/86

1. Discrimination among environmental sounds   —   —   —   —
2. Discrimination among sounds that rhyme   —   —   —   —
3. Discrimination among beginning consonant sounds   —   —   —   —
4. Discrimination among beginning vowel sounds   —   —   —   —
5. Discrimination among beginning consonant blends   —   —   —   —

ADDITION

1. One digit plus 1   —   —   —   —
2. One digit plus 0   —   —   —   —
3. One digit plus one digit   —   —   —   —

TIME

1. Can tell time by daily activities   —   —   —   —
2. Can tell time by hour   —   —   —   —
3. Knows that the small hand represents hours   —   —   —   —
4. Knows that the large hand represents minutes   —   —   —   —
5. Can tell time by the half hour   —   —   —   —

CODE : √ — Using skill well; N — Need practice; I — Improving in use; R — Reteach

---

identified and used to track student growth and development. As students progress into the upper years of school, specific skills for special concepts are designed for each student according to his God-given abilities, gifts, and interest levels. At the elementary levels, all students work through primary skills which deal with the nature of man as God designed him to perform. For example, all primary students are taught basic reading skills because in doing this they fulfill the biblical command to "study to show thyself approved unto God, a workman that needeth not to be ashamed, rightly divining the word of truth" (II Tim 2:15). Secondary students build on these basic skills by emphasizing the development of high skill performances in specialty subject spheres and by cultivating their God-given ministry interests or talent areas. "For so we

have many members [students] in one body [school], and all
members have not the same office, . . . having then gifts
differing according to the grace that is given to us," (Romans
12:4,6).

In addition to recording skill achievements in academic or
physical areas, there are other areas of student development that
need to be evaluated. There are social, emotional, ethical,
cognitive and confessional areas of human development.
Students develop in these areas while under direct teacher
supervision. Therefore, teachers and parents must help students
shape their character development in accordance with biblical
standards.

One procedure for monitoring these areas of development is
to have teachers write their observations and recommendations.
Teachers ought to write short paragraphs for each area, then
meet with the parents in order to orally review their findings.
Suggested conference guidelines follow.

PARENT—TEACHER CONFERENCE GUIDELINES[34]

I. SOCIAL DEVELOPMENT

    A. relates well with others in work and play

    B. relates well with teacher

    C. is sensitive to the feelings of others

    D. understands his own feelings

    E. is able to make friends

II. EMOTIONAL DEVELOPMENT

    A. shows evidence of being able to work with feelings of anger,frustration, and
       disappointment

    B. has a good self—concept

    C. takes responsibility to make decisions

    D. can handle criticism by others

III. ETHICAL DEVELOPMENT

    A. demonstrates care for others

    B. shows respect for authority, *i.e.* teacher, Bible

    C. shows respect for the property of others

    D. shows sensitivity for God's demands

    E. shows sensitivity for the Holy Spirit

IV. CONFESSIONAL DEVELOPMENT

    A. demonstrates a sense of being called to serve God

    B. comprehends a sense of his place in God's plan

    C. able to respond to the Biblical message and shows evidence in daily life

    D. shows evidence of personal relationship with God

V. COGNITIVE DEVELOPMENT

    A. enjoys a range of difficulty and can deal with it

    B. completes assignments

    C. sees work done as a response to his Creator

    D. able to follow directions

    E. is attentive

    F. can work independent of constant teacher help

    G. working at ability levels

---

d. Custom-made Curriculum

In order to be consistent with biblical teaching, a personalized curriculum must be constructed for each student. The Spirit of God makes covenant children according to the personal plan that God devised before the foundation of the world (I Cor 12:4-31; Eph 1). Unique gifts are specially designed and given by God to every student. Various learning rates, needs and capacities are possessed by students. Distinguishing interests are held by individual students. Family history and current life-context or environment vary for every student. For example, we found it difficult to get Bobby, a second year student, to write stories. Since writing skills are biblical and we emphasize them early, it was our goal to have him write. Although Bobby has the ability to write short stories, he resisted our efforts. One day he was given a kitten which he named Tom. Tom became integral to Bobby's life, and we found that Bobby would readily write stories about Tom even though he preferred not to write about Spot, Jane or Dick. The book characters were unreal, abstract and irrelevant to Bobby. Tom was real, easily visualized and close to Bobby's heart. While writing about Tom, Bobby learned spelling, grammar, penmanship, and thinking and communication skills. Boredom and unnecessary repetition was exchanged for positive emotional motivation and Spirit direction for the glory of God because his written stories can be collected, bound and used as reading books for other students.

Biblical Christian school curriculum must be adaptable. It must be able to accomodate the diverse and multiform working of the Spirit of God in the lives of His children. Some students are given much, so much is required. Other students are from split homes or are adopted or have been abused. Students who come from mature Christian homes differ from students whose families are new to the things of God. These and numerous other considerations must be a part of a Christian school's curriculum plan.

Custom-made curriculum hangs upon the skill achievement framework. The skills provide structure for individualized curriculum. Although the skills, to be achieved, are fixed because of their biblical nature or due to their adherence to God's creation laws, the teaching methods, the resources used and the learning context may be different for each student. Students can progress in reading skills by reading different books at their God-given rate of reading. Why must every student read the same book and work from the same page? Is it for teacher convenience or to meet student needs? Consider Melody. She is a kindergarten student with above average reading skill. She has a strong desire to read basal readers. During her first school year she read all kind of basal readers for grades one through three. Her skill level allowed her to read and comprehend many stories each day. Yes, she is gifted, but we believe that every student is gifted uniquely by the grace of God.

Recently I visited a fifth grade classroom. There were twenty-five desks lined up in five equal rows. On every desk was a copy of the same textbook and each book was opened to the same page. Every student was to be doing the same assignment in the same time period. Does this take into account the biblical teaching about the nature of the learner or the nature of learning? The Spirit of God does not mass produce nor mass educate His people as machines produce pennies at the United States mint. Biblical educators must take this into account.

The curriculum is custom-made for each student when the teacher and student are given the freedom to choose reading books which are correlated with the student's individual learning context and the student's reading skill achievement level. The same is true when applied to spelling, grammar, mathematics, vocabulary, thinking or any skill area. In fact, genuine custom-tailored curriculum will make this correlation in all the skill areas for every student. Furthermore, this individualization becomes vivid when the student integrally relates the skills in a unit of study and when the skills are developed into projects and then into personal acts of ministry.

Custom-made curriculum must be flexible. Teachers may say that custom-made curriculum is "ideal" but can never be implemented in the classroom. It seems impossible to have twenty or more students in several different grades, all working on different skills at the same time. How can a teacher supervise all this activity and still provide instruction? When will the teacher have time to prepare lesson plans for each student?

Teachers and parents must understand that students may be put in groups of ten or less to learn a given skill. The basic skills for elementary student development are the same for most students. It is the students who are vastly different. Curriculum is personalized for them when the teacher permits each student to develop the skills in his own learning context. Both the teacher and the student are freed from curriculum dominance to give scope to each student's rate of learning, life-context, personal interests, God-given gifts and the Spirit's direction for life ministry. Skills and individual characteristics are related in God's plan for each student in a flexible relationship which is reciprocal and supplementary. It may seem like a struggle but actually this relationship enhances student learning. (See illustration below.)

This illustration shows individual students being grouped to study one specific skill, yet the students' personal interests are included. Teachers should realize that unlimited activities, exercises, experiences, curriculum materials, teaching aids and books are at their disposal to facilitate personal skill development, to unfold God's gifts and are to be utilized for ministry projects. The customized curriculum column stands in a reciprocal and supplementary relationship with the skill column, just as concrete ideas stand in a similar relationship with abstract ideas. In the learning process, the customized curriculum column represents a personalized and relevant concrete basis for abstract skills. Abstract skills not only find their right meaning in their relationship to their Creator but also, for each student, they will be manifest in a God-honoring, relevant life-context.

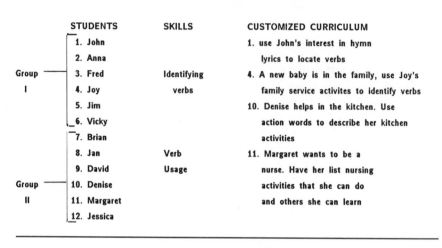

In order to give direction to students, teachers develop daily work assignment notes for each student. This task does not require much time, but it does necessitate a vivid relationship with every student. It is good for teachers to begin to work together with individuals or groups to compose their assignments. For example, assignment notes for Grace, Kristen and Doug could read as follows:

STUDENT ASSIGNMENT NOTES

ASSIGNMENTS	OBJECTIVES
Personal reading	from books of their own choosing, in preparation for prepositional phrase skills
Write story for newspaper	stories may be about the unit topic or another topic while specific punctuation skills are being worked on
Book reports	students will write and orally present to each other a report from the book being read; reading comprehension skills and oral communication skills are developed
Ministry project	individual ministry projects are to be worked on independently or in groups
9:35, meet with teacher*	teacher will review work and give specific skill instruction

* At times, a group of students will meet at the same time. Each student has a regularly scheduled personal time with the teacheŕ.

The above assignment may last for up to two hours. On the left side of this assignment sheet, students receive directive information. In a short time, students will know what they are to do with each assignment, because at their meetings, the teacher will explain what is expected. The information in the right column may be known by the students from previous meetings with the teacher or be mentally noted by the teacher as teaching objectives. While students work on their assignments independently or in groups, the teacher supervises by rotating from student to student, or meets with specific students according to the day's schedule. Parent's may be actively incorporated into this process as aides. They can be used as supervisors, helpers, participants within the learning process, listeners, and observers for practice and drill work. Below is a sample aide schedule.

AIDE SCHEDULE
(written by Don McMillan)

8:30—8:45	Help K's and 1st with journals
8:45—9:00	Listen to Justin read
9:00—9:15	Listen to Shelly read
9:15—9:30	Assist K's with books
9:30—9:45	Listen to Elizabeth read
10:00	Supervise break for K—2
10:20	Sit in on devotions for 3—6
10:45	Help with P.E. or music
11:30—11:45	Supervise 2nd grade math skill work
11:45—12:00	Take a break
12:00—1:00	Supervise lunch and recess

By the fourth year in school, with minor teacher management, most students will be able to write their own daily class assignments. Students will know how to regularly include spelling, cursive practice or specific language skill exercises. Teachers will be directive with specific skill instruction in mathematics, primary phonics, and by suggesting various learning activities.

Further daily assignments are illustrated below:

Jessica	James
—write in your journal	—write in your journal
—do pages 18 & 19 in the orange book	—do questions for Fire Safety Tips
—read to Mrs. Kearney at 8:55	—do sheets 83 and 84
—do pages 42 and 43 in worldly wise	—read Mrs. Piggle—Wiggle
	—meet with Mrs. Smeal

Skills, projects and service ministries are all part of one cohesive unit, like "Sea Animals," "Trees," or "Community." Teachers control student individualization by keeping the student's work within the bounds of the unit topic or their family context which are to lead directly to service-ministry objectives. Control is also maintained by constantly evaluating each student's acquisition of skills. Students may not dwell on skills that they have mastered or proceed into skill areas that are beyond their ability level.

e. Freedom and Discipline

On the surface, the concepts of freedom and discipline appear to be opposites or antithetical. This is not true. Biblical educators believe that freedom and discipline work in a harmonious fashion. They stand, as other aspects of integral curriculum, in a reciprocal and harmonious relationship. It is based squarely on the Triune Creator. God created biblical freedom and biblical discipline. Thus, they do not work against each other, nor are they independent or autonomous from each other.

Nevertheless, it seems that unbiblical discipline reigns as tyranny in many Christian schools. Without biblical discipline, anarchy would reign. On the other hand, we must be careful not to reduce biblical freedom to an abstract word which never takes place in the classroom. It would be hypocritical to claim that "Christ has made us free, and not entangled again with the yoke of bondage" (Gal 5:1), if our classroom structure is so strict that no true freedom exists. Consequently, we believe that covenant students must be given the opportunity to freely make biblically responsible decisions. Students ought to be given a variety of choices during the school day and the freedom to carry out the choice and experience consequences.

The freedom to make choices is not an unlimited freedom. Biblical educational freedom is found in God's law. For covenant students, God's law is the environment of life.[35] Accordingly, biblical discipline is directed by biblical law for "the Law has become our schoolmaster to bring us to Christ" (Gal 3:24). We, therefore, contend that biblical freedom and discipline are naturally related such that one directly implies or is complementary to the other. Both concepts must operate harmoniously in biblical Christian schools.

Gary Bridges, author of *The Pursuit of Holiness,* illustrates this principle. He says that the exercise of real choices between the pursuit of holiness and the pursuit of wickedness enables a person or student to become, over time and through a series of choices, experts in holiness or wickedness. A series of Spirit-directed, biblically right choices leads to holy character (Rom 6:19). This requires the freedom to make real choices. Students cannot have all their choices chosen for them by teachers or curriculum writers because it will rob them of the opportunity to develop an internal discipline or training which is necessary for true Christian living. The strength to make right choices is given by God through the inworking of the Holy Spirit who directs students to biblical responsibility (I Thes 4:9). Therefore, there is a proper balance between biblical freedom for choice and biblical responsibility. Both must be operating simultaneously in the Christian teaching-learning process. In brief, human responsibility and God's enablement go hand-in-hand. Christian teachers, using their personal rules or publishers' curriculum to uphold their students responsibilities, deprive them of the opportunity for God to work through their choices to build biblical responsibility (Col 1:29; Ps 127:1; Neh 4:9). Bridges points out that the outworking of this dual operation is through prayer. Prayer acknowledges dependency upon God in order for students to exercise biblical freedom of choice (Neh 1:4 and 2:4).[36]

Let us clarify this by using an example from within our home or family context. We have two children. One child has a piece of cake while the other has nothing to eat. Our hope is that the child with the cake will share it with his little sister. We could tell him that he must share the cake which means that he has no freedom or choice. He must share. We could say, "Son, wouldn't you like to share the cake with your sister?" In this case, our question appears to give him the freedom to say "No!"; but he knows from our tone of voice, our authoritative expectation, and from past experiences that the "No" option is not really there. Accordingly, he says, "Yes," to please his parents or due to resignation to the truth that there is no real choice. On the other hand, we could ask the same question in a learning environment where the "No" option is real. Suppose he does say "No!" When this happens, we discuss with him what the Bible teaches us about giving, sharing and loving. We also allow his "No" answer to stand. If the Holy Spirit does not convict him to share, then, in some cases, we will not require him to do so. To be sure, we will pray for him and with him about biblical sharing, but we do not remove from him the freedom to make a real choice. We pray that the Spirit of God will graciously turn his heart, that the "No" answers will turn into "Yes" answers, and that the internalized conviction to share will root deeply in his heart and be exemplified in his character. When frequent "Yes" answers are given, we will have reason to believe that our prayers have been answered. We will then be able to proceed with giving him more freedom because God has enabled him to practice biblical responsibility. Gradually, with the Spirit of God working over the course of many years and through many developing experiences with freedom and choice, our children will learn to live in accord with biblical freedom and discipline.

The above family example does not mean that parents or teachers are to condone sin. The plain truth is that they do sin. Parents and teachers must carefully guide and nurture students toward biblical holiness and away from sin. The idea is similar to how God deals with every Christian. Through the work of His Spirit and the clear direction revealed in the Bible, He directs us toward holiness while requiring responsible biblical freedom. Without compromising His sovereignty or holiness, God gives His people the real choice to sin or to affirm our stand in our Lord and Savior, Jesus Christ.

* * * * *

To demonstrate biblical freedom and discipline operating harmoniously in the Christian school classroom, the following examples are given:

1. Billy is a student having a problem with personal responsibility. He wants to sit next to his best friend, Sammy. "We won't fool around," claims Billy. Sammy says, "Please, pretty

please; we will do all our work!" The skeptical Mrs. Jones gives them the freedom to sit as they have requested, but before she leaves, she warns them that unwarranted disruption or lack of work will result in the loss of this freedom. Despite the pleas for a second opportunity, within fifteen minutes, Mrs. Jones must move Billy's desk to another area of the room because the boys disrupted one another. Their freedom was structured by the biblical principle to accomplish, in an orderly fashion, their God-given tasks for the day. By breaking the law they lost their freedom.

Freedom Principle: In order to develop biblical responsibility, the student must be given the freedom to choose from among non-biblical and biblical alternatives and experience the consequences. Biblical freedom of action must result in biblical consequences.

2. Janet is normally a hard working and successful student. However, while working on a difficult fraction concept her emotions take control. In tears, she exclaims, "I hate school!" Her teacher, Mrs. McMillan, gives Janet the freedom to express her emotions but does not ignore the outburst. Together they sit down, calm down and begin to examine appropriate emotional responses to frustration. In some cases of inappropriate emotional behavior, physical correction may be needed; in other instances, biblical nurturing may prove effective.

Freedom Principle: To experience and express emotions biblically, students must be given the freedom to express emotion, even when they are expressed inappropriately. Both biblical and unbiblical expressions of emotion need to be addressed by teachers.

3. Tom is an outstanding student. He is able to handle abstract number concepts when direction is given. His teacher, Mrs. Pugh, realizes that Paul, a classmate, learns quickly when he handles concrete objects in order to learn abstract concepts. He cannot comprehend abstract concepts without them. Holly learns these concepts simply by reading about them. She is able to visualize the concrete objects without teacher direction or by exploring with hands on learning. These three students are disciplined to learn the basic concepts or skills required because

they are required of them in order to properly understand arithmetic. The teacher is given the freedom to choose the best learning activity or method for each student. Sometimes students may have the freedom to choose their own preferred learning method, while teachers must be free to provide various learning experiences for different students.

Freedom Principle: Education is enhanced when students and teachers are free to choose preferred learning methods and learning contexts.

4. Donna and David have recently learned how to figure the price per pound for grocery products. They have learned this new skill in order to serve God by serving others. As part of their Ministry-Learning curriculum, Donna helps her mother purchase the best buys at the grocery store; David helps his dad calculate the price for a large amount of nails he is buying. Students are disciplined to willingly serve God while retaining the freedom to choose their ministry application.

Freedom Principle: The biblical interpretation of skills and facts or Christian understanding becomes personally relevant and God-glorifying when students are given an opportunity to choose aspects of the teaching-learning process which allows them to minister to or serve others. Dictating to students what their ministry is going to be restricts student sensitivity to Spirit-consciousness. It creates a false crutch, which will not be present during adult years, for discerning God's gifts and His plan for their life of biblical ministry. Students must serve God and we must give them biblical freedom to minister with their God-given gifts.

* * * * *

The key point is that Christian educators and parents want God's children to *internalize* biblical freedom and discipline. Students are to behave according to biblical law and within the freedom Christ has provided because in their hearts they believe that their actions are the right things to do. We want students to act biblically out of inner conviction which is a specialized work of the Holy Spirit. The Spirit of God works in the hearts of regenerate students to incline them, by the grace of God, to will to do the will of God. This is internalized, God-conscious, biblical discipline as students exercise responsible freedom in accord with the covenant God has established with them. It is not to be fear or terror, whereby students are forced to obey. Rather, we desire to develop an atmosphere where God's Spirit stimulates His covenant students to do rightly because they love Him in response to God first loving them.

f. Classrooms

A *Washington Post* writer, T.R. Reid, reports that the one-room school is "enjoying a modest but unmistakable revival . . . [with] emphasis on basics, individual instruction and a deliberate mixing of the grades and ages, so older students help teach their younger brethren - and learn from repetition."[37]

We advocate a school atmosphere which has some of the characteristics of the old, one-room school. While rejecting the harshness and oppression which often accompanied Nineteenth Century schools, we embrace a Christian family orientation and home-like atmosphere where the students are loved and respected. On a daily basis, students may receive appropriate hugs or signs of affection, and frequently, each student is talked *with*, not talked *at*.

The classroom characteristics of the mid-Twentieth Century are artificial. Relationships in modern classrooms are unnatural substitutes in contrast to the real world where people live, work, worship and socialize. They are synthetic deceptions for culture. They remind me of zoo exhibits where bears, lions or monkeys are kept in caged or walled areas that look like their natural environment. Everyone knows that the seal pool is far too small; that the hippopotamus barely fits in his pond, a sad substitute for the Nile River; and that the real trees behind the gorilla pen make it home-like but are outside his playful reach. Modern zookeepers are significantly improving their exhibit habitates while educators have made little progress in the past hundred years.

Classrooms are designed for the abstract thinking of adults and children, who are not adults in their thinking or behavior, are expected to behave like adults. Twenty-five to thirty-five students quietly sitting in rows or squares in a self-contained room is not the ordinary way of life for children. Children need to have a classroom which is the home base to their extended classroom, *their community:* government offices, libraries, parks, factories, churches, homes, recreation areas, business offices, shopping malls, and all other service areas. The classroom, itself, ought to be a base of operations and a hub of activity. Students are in the classroom to be taught skills, to practice or drill, to research and to build projects. Consequently, the classroom has work tables, computers, desks, innumerable supplies, books, and learning aids of all types. In addition, the classroom has a cushioned sofa and pillowed chairs on a rug in a homey corner of the room for leisure reading. It is a place where students make noise, enjoy each other, create messes, think of ways to solve problems, have free time and sing and pray together. There are quiet times for concentrated study, and times for teacher instruction. To be sure, it is a place where students minister one to another.

In our school, students are not packaged into grades. It may appear to be a school where students in different grades are taught together, but we do not consider the students to be in any given grade. We simply track how many years a student has attended school. Starting at age six, all students are in their first year of school. Students do not *pass* or *fail* a year in school. Rather, we closely monitor their educational development by using the Skill Achievement Records. They progress as God enables them. Students graduate when they have mastered the skills necessary to advance into college, to enter a trade or to work in some field of ministry. Recently I watched finals of the TV program, *Jeopardy.* High school students were competing for scholarships. The finalists had eliminated thousands of other students. Only the top three remained. After demonstrating their knowledge by answering several difficult questions, the contestants were introduced. One was going to Harvard, another to Yale, and the last back to high school. My heart sank. What could a traditional high school offer this brilliant young woman that was worth a year of her life? Everyone could see that she was more than ready to advance beyond a series of courses which measure out 45 minute doses of fragmented material.

The classroom is not a factory system. Six-year-old students are not pressured like salesmen for commission sales, or a basketball player trying to convert a game winning free throw. We enjoy the individuality of each student and respect their thinking. Artificial group development schedules are not set up; the entire class is not crammed with grade-by-grade facts and skills. The needs of individual students are more important than the curriculum program. "We push the 'slow' and bore the 'quick',"[38] says Susan Schaeffer Macaulay, when students are expected to learn according to a non-personal, curriculum schedule and not according to individual ability. Just as God sanctifies the individual lives of His people, teachers, guided by the Spirit of God, are to develop lessons that are structured and fitted to each child's need - when each is ready and at each one's level and speed.[39] Although biblical standards are expected, students should not feel that they are lagging behind or are superior to other children. Consequently, students are not learning in a classroom pressure-cooker. Rather, students learn in an atmosphere where they are encouraged to responsibly care for their own learning needs and to work under pressure which is regulated by their individual ability levels.

We believe that students of various grade levels ought to be mixed together in one classroom. Each teacher is primarily responsible for twenty students which represent a range of three or four years of schooling. For example, our primary teachers would have a mixture of students from the first year to the third year in school while our middle school teachers would have students from the fourth year to the sixth year in school. Regularly, primary and middle school students would be mixed for learning or ministry activities. There is a great deal of flexibility with this arrangement which will allow for us to meet specific student needs or to take advantage of unique teaching talents. There are distinct advantages to this arrangement. Examine the following:

1. Older students are given ample opportunity to minister to and serve the younger students.

2. Teachers are challenged with a variety of student levels which keeps them fresh, rather than stagnating by teaching the same material year after year.

3. Students stay with the same teacher for many years. This enables teachers to nurture specific students from their early learning activities through the middle school years. A deep sense of accomplishment is thereby achieved; less time is wasted by students and teachers adjusting to one another; lifetime personal relationships are fostered; long term in loco parentis is established, which is in keeping with family-type relationships; and teacher-parent alliances become stronger.

4. Younger students are able to learn from older students, by example and through direct affiliation.

5. Students needing extra time in the primary areas may easily stay in their primary group for extra help while regularly being with the middle school group for other activities. Other students may be able to work with a middle school group without spending less time in the primary group. They could easily be assigned to this group while frequently doing activities with primary students. Therefore, because students are ordinarily in a mixed grade environment, it is easier to individualize their curriculum and "failure" stigma or pride factors are reduced.

g. The Teacher and the Teaching Environment

The teaching is fast-paced. The teacher must be flexible, patient, creative and skill conscious. Above all, the suppositions discussed in Part II must have permeated the heart of the teacher and must be absolute guides for all of life and teaching. The teacher must love and respect children. The ability to get on the thinking level of each student is fundamental. The teacher must be of notable quality. "The teacher must be a man [person] of the highest aims, and of the highest moral qualifications." and, thus, held in highest honor. "It [is] one of life's greatest privileges to be a teacher, because . . . it [is] a great privilege to teach a child the law."[40] Christian teachers ought to be people who are endowed with teaching gifts from God and who are highly trained since they are to teach the children of the King of kings.

Teachers must know the skills to be acquired by students. Developmental skills ought to be thoroughly understood by all teachers. They need a solid grasp of the basic learning content found in a liberal arts education. Teachers must be skilled in providing innumerable learning experiences, which enable students to acquire skills and factual content in a biblical context.

A skilled teacher is like a skilled salesperson. For example, a skilled computer salesperson knows all the features of his computer products. Computer operation, usage, software, potential, limits, compatibility, service and repair are all areas of a salesperson's expertise. A competent computer salesperson knows the details of his product line. He knows computer language; reads current journals on computer innovations; continues his computer education; and is recognized as a computer expert by his peers. Anyone can sell computers, even without computer literacy, but it is the skilled salesperson that we want when we make computer purchases. It is the skilled salesperson who will successfully deal in computers. Similarly, anyone can teach, but it is the teacher who knows developmental skills, learning content and creative learning activities, and who successfully teaches, that I want for my children. Teachers who know reading skills, math skills, language skills and a host of skills in all other areas will be able to give individualized instruction to many students while untrained teachers and their students are slaves to curriculum publishers.

The teacher's class management is like a busy stage director's with actors, runners, musicians, costume personnel, make-up specialists and numerous others involved in producing a play. It is like being a coach with defensive and offensive players, game strategy, scouting reports, practice time, game scheduling, referees, fans, and parent involvement. In both of these illustrations, the stage director and the coach are simultaneously involved with many spheres of activity, and they must hold them together in an integral relationship. Teaching is similar because the teacher simultaneously manages numerous students at various skill levels with differing, yet personal, learning contexts. In a traditional educational system student differences may be ignored, made light of, or covered over by textbook busy work; nonetheless individuality exists in every classroom. In contrast, in Ministry-Learning, individuals and specific groups of students receive instruction and supervision. Classroom control is sustained while student freedom is preserved. Parent-teachers receive guidance and direction, and ministry projects and actual ministry activities are kept before everyone. The teacher talks to a group of students, moves from individual to individual, suggests ideas, checks resource books, nurtures, corrects, listens and supervises projects and ministry activities.

This whirlwind of activity surrounding the teacher may seem like chaos to the untrained eye. Control may seem to be nonexistent, and it will be for the incompetent teacher. This is one of the main objectives for the Freedom and Discipline section: to teach students to behave responsibly. Responsible students talk with each other by sharing a learning experience, a new idea, an interesting book or helpful hints. They may choose to change learning activities while being accountable for their daily learning tasks. Every student in the classroom may be involved in a different activity, but each one knows his duty and his limits. The class management procedures are well known by the teacher and all the students.

In the typical Christian home, the father may be repairing an appliance; mother may be preparing a picnic lunch; the children may be reading or talking on the phone or building a toy model. This home is not in chaos even though five different activities are taking place. Each family member is free to do a personal task while remaining within biblical bounds and established family order. Excessive noise, accidents, misbehavior or problems may disrupt the family coherence and need to be addressed. So it is in our classroom environment. The teacher supervises many learning activities while students are involved with numerous, changing, learning experiences.

To understand this view of the teaching environment, teachers must realize that classroom control is not defined by students who are quiet and who are bound to their desks. Even though there are times when discipline and correction are needed, the school environment, like the home, should not be oppressive. Both the classroom and home should be cheerful, happy places. Spankings, disciplinary action and instruction are an important part of the biblical teaching-learning process, but God's grace, forgiveness, mercy and loving kindness are also vital. These things should be the hallmark of our Christian classroom environment.

Teachers are responsible for creating this classroom environment. A pleasant teaching environment doesn't just happen. It takes work, example, and clear instruction. Every teacher must work out an organizational plan for the classroom; classroom procedures, file systems, assigned shelving for supplies, time schedules and places for personal belongings, all need to be arranged. Teachers must be living examples of God's grace, of Christian friendliness, and of the biblical work ethic. Then, with careful instruction and clear communication, they can set up a teaching environment which is honorable to God.

The teaching environment in the integral Christian school goes far beyond the school classroom. It includes the home, church and community. Teachers need to have a grasp of the home life of each student. This will facilitate the creation of personal learning activities and establish a personal context for the acquisition of new skills and facts. If David's daddy is a traveling computer consultant, while Nathan's daddy is a local pastor, their home-teaching environments will be different. These differences are true of all families, and teachers must know them and make allowances for them.

Furthermore, the teaching environment must include the entire school community, county, state and, in some cases, the region of the country. By the senior year in school, students need to be in the community teaching environment more than they are in the academic classroom environment. Primary youth need to be in a school with a home-like teaching environment more than in the academic classroom environment; middle school students need an academic classroom teaching environment to obtain skills and facts. A good teacher is one who is well aware of the events, services, ministry activities and leadership of his local community, and is instrumental in getting students actively involved for the glory of God.

The community teaching environment for upper school students requires knowledgeable teachers, responsible students and transportation. The teacher's knowledge and authoritative position are not enough. Student's must act responsibly, that is, their intention and actions must be in harmony with biblical principles for Christian living. To achieve this, teachers must prepare primary and middle school students by giving them appropriate responsibilities so that they are prepared to assume greater responsibilities in upper school. For example, middle school students may be given the responsibility to lead groups, solve quarrels, produce and supervise classroom ministry projects, compose official school letters and newspaper articles, submit to student leaders or implement a task with certain time restraints. These activities are designed to prepare younger students for greater responsibilities, such as driving cars, apprenticeship experiences, and large-scale personal or group ministry activities. This is the whole point for our Freedom and Discipline section. By gradually teaching students to be biblically responsible with seemingly little deeds, then they will be better prepared to biblically manage larger ministries. There is no shortage of community resources or community ministry opportunities.

The integralist school's community learning environment is the real world where people live. We propose that our students be gradually nurtured as they begin to take their place in the world. Students should not be kept for twelve or thirteen years in the greenhouse atmosphere of a school where teachers artificially attempt to prepare them for actual life! We must teach our students to swim as Christians in God's real world by gradually placing them in the water, teaching them to swim, instructing them about water safety rules and exposing them to various swimming ministries. This is far better than hypothetically talking about the real world of swimming in water while remaining in a dry classroom. Traditionally educated students are pushed into the pool of the real world for the first time at graduation. They must either sink or swim. Many sink because the Spirit of God has not had a biblical school system to use for His glory.

The integralist Christian teaching environment is a genuine challenge which incorporates the entire pattern of God's world. Teachers in this environment are released from mechanical repetition. They do not use the same textbook or teaching activity with every student. They present a continuing stream of differing texts and activities to students according to their needs, abilities and interests. For example, while studying the Revolutionary War, our students read about it from several different textbooks, reference works, novels and from each others' writings. One history textbook, which limits us to one publisher's view is not enough. Consequently, a wide variety of materials were used and greater factual content was acquired by all our students. No one textbook is used, except the Bible. A student may specialize in a certain area of colonial life, which is of personal interest, while all the students obtain general data, from a wide variety of sources, concerning the war and their own personal interest areas. Teachers, then, serve as aides, resource persons, creators of ideas, supervisors, evaluation guides and coordinators. They lead the students in discussions and group analysis activities.

This teaching environment creates a close, personal relationship between teachers and students. It is the natural result of a customized curriculum. Much one-on-one time between a student and a teacher results in an understanding or rapport which enhances the teaching-learning process, and is gratifying. Such close relationships are rewarding and often longstanding. Teachers will find great joy and contentment as they work with students and observe the hand of God upon them, as they develop and are used as His instruments, for His glory, in His world-ministry.

h. Parent-Teacher Aides

Parents want to be directly involved with the teaching of their children. It is biblical for parents to be actively involved in teaching their children in Christian classrooms. We believe that parents, guided by teachers, ought to be regularly involved in the instructional process in their children's classroom. This means that parents are part of the school's teaching team and not simply relegated to stacking library books, driving for field trips, doing clerical work or acting as class party chairpersons. There is a home-school partnership embeded in the ministry-learning teaching process.

The popular home-schooling movement demonstrates that many parents want this intimate involvement. In fact, many traditional schools have adopted programs to work in cooperation with home-schooling families and several curriculum publishers produce a variety of educational materials for home-schools. Local home-school groups have formed to encourage each other, hold conferences, defend themselves against government interference and share ideas.

Educational researchers have statistical evidence to support the belief that parent involvement helps children learn more effectively. "What parents do to help their children learn is more important to academic success than how well-off the family is."[41] We believe that this help does not stop at the classroom door, or at age 5 or 6.

The Bible teaches that the education of children is the responsibility of the home. Integral Christian education works in harmony with this biblical teaching. Parents are not restricted from our classroom. We encourage them to be present and to work with all the students. This is not the usual practice in traditional classrooms. Parents are rarely, if ever, present in them, except at Open House or to attend athletic events. Most teachers are fearful of parents, supervisors, or visitors in *their* classrooms. Often they feel threatened or uncomfortable with such outsiders in the room. Biblical classrooms, however, include direct parental involvement in the teaching-learning process.

How shall parents be involved? A suggested aide schedule and a few examples have been given. However, before parent-aides invade the classroom, they must be oriented to the teaching-learning system, understand the class procedures, and observe the teaching-learning process. Before school begins, teachers need to teach parents and prepare them for teaching service. After a few weeks of school, when students settle down into the teaching-learning system, the teacher introduces the parent-teachers into the classroom to observe and to provide elementary teaching activities. Gradually they are given additional responsibilities and teaching tasks while under teacher supervision. In a short time, parents feel comfortable in the classroom and their children, too, are comfortable with their parents being present. Quickly, parent-aides are able to learn and follow time schedules which list their numerous teaching activities.

Teachers need to set up a monthly calendar for their aides. Some parents can serve weekly, bi-weekly or even daily. They may assist all day or half a day. We try to schedule aides so that there is always one present to help the teacher, but the number of aides at any given time is dependent upon the teacher's class situation or ability. In addition, we cannot expect each parent to assist in the same way. Individual parent-aide schedules need to be made for each helper. Separate aide schedules can be made to maximize the use of particular parent talents and to allow the teacher a way to alter his personal schedule.

Some parent-teacher activities are as follows:

1. read stories to students;

2. listen to individual students read stories;

3. guide students in class or group devotions;

4. lead students in singing activities;

5. drill students with flash cards;

6. supervise students during independent study and answer their questions;

7. guide students in practicing particular skills, e.g., cursive writing;

8. give spelling reviews with immediate assessment;

9. assist students in working through a ministry project;

10. counsel students by talking and listening to them;

11. introduce a new skill concept to an individual or group;

12. direct small group learning activities, e.g., working with pattern blocks, skill games for physical development;

13. lead book review discussions, political debates or history discourses

14. supervise community-classroom service activities;

15. listen to speeches for delivery skills, word pronunciation, clarity, accuracy and eloquence.

Parent-teacher aides do enhance student achievement. They improve one-on-one, tutor-type, learning situations; they detect individual learning difficulties for teachers to nurture; they free the teacher to handle difficult problems or to do advance planning for individual students; and they strengthen the home-school relationship. Clearly there are many tasks that parent-teachers can perform in every classroom. Moreover, their children receive the direct benefit from such ministries.

Parent-teacher aides must be careful not to do the student's work. This is a real temptation. Aides are to help or assist students. They are to be ministering servants to the students by nurturing them. It is not helping students if a parent-teacher gives predetermined answers or performs skill tasks for the students. Students may need encouragement, directions clarified or a prompting suggestion, but they also need to do their own cutting, coloring, counting, dissecting or writing with their own words.

NOTES

1. M. M. Krappen Tudor Puritanism (Chicago: University of Chicago Press, 1939) pp. 473-474.

2. A. A. Baker The Successful Christian School, p.42.

3. Peter B. De Boer Shifts in Curriculum Theory for Christian Education (Grand Rapids, MI: Calvin College, 1983) p.9.

4. John Dewey Experience and Education (London: Collier Books, 1963) pp.17-18.

5. Peter B. DeBoer Shifts in Curriculum Theory, p.16.

6. John Dewey Experience and Education, p.19-20.

7. Peter F. Drucker The Age of Discontinuity: Guidelines to Our Changing Society (New York: Harper & Row, 1969) p.340.

8. Daryl Borquist *Striving for Renascence in Education,* unpublished speech, Continental Congress on the Christian World View II, Dallas, TX, July 23, 1985.

9. Cornelius Jaarsma (ed.) Fundamentals in Christian Education (Grand Rapids, MI: Eerdmans, 1953) p.293.

10. Peter B. De Boer Shifts in Curriculum Theory for Christian Education, p.18.

11. *Ibid.,* p.23

12. *Ibid.,* p.21.

13. Nicholas Wolterstorff Curriculum: By What Standard? (Grand Rapids, MI: Christian Schools International, 1966) p.1-16.

14. Geraldine Steensma, personal letter, January, 1986.

15. Geraldine Steensma Shaping School Curriculum: A Biblical View (Middleburg Heights, OH: Signal Publishing Co., 1977) p.7.

16. *Ibid.*, p.16.

17. Jay Adams BACK TO THE BLACKBOARD, p.88.

18. *Ibid.*, p.90-91.

19. *Ibid.*, p.107-108.

20. *Ibid.*, p.111.

21. Quoted from promotional materials for Pittsburg Urban Christian School, Pittsburg, PA.

22. Geraldine J. Steensma SHAPING SCHOOL CURRICULUM INTEGRAL LEARNING: A BIBLICAL VIEW (Middleburg Heights, OH: Signal Publishing Co., 1984) p.1.

23. *Ibid.*

24. *Ibid.*

25. Alta Vista College *Alta Vista Homeschool Curriculum Parents' Handbook* (Medina, WA: Alta Vista College, 1985)pp.I-10, I-11.

26. Geraldine J. Steensma SHAPING SCHOOL CURRICULUM, p.15.

27. *Ibid.*, p.30.

28. *Ibid.*, p.23.

29. *Ibid.*, pp.6-7.

30. Paul Springstubb *How to vaccinate students against thinking*, THE PLAIN DEALER, April 18, 1987, p.9A.

31. Jay Adams BACK TO THE BLACKBOARD, pp.115-124.

32. Paul Springstubb, *How to vaccinate students against thinking.*

33. *Elementary Skill Records* (Middleburg Heights, OH: Signal Publishing Co., 1984).

34. *Ibid.*

35. Rousas Jon Rushdoony THE ONE AND THE MANY: STUDIES IN THE PHILOSOPHY OF ORDER AND ULTIMACY (Fairfax, VA: Thoburn Press, 1978) p.33.

36. Gerald Bridges Public address held during the meetings of Grace Covenant Fellowship, Parma Hts., OH, April, 1987.

37. T. R. Reid *One-room school back: its time to listen up,* THE PLAIN DEALER, Cleveland, OH, October 6, 1985, p.18.

38. Susan Shaeffer Macaulay FOR THE CHILDREN'S SAKE: FOUNDATIONS OF EDUCATION FOR HOME AND SCHOOL (Westchester, IL: Crossway Books, 1984) p.149.

39. *Ibid.,* p.28.

40. William Barclay EDUCATIONAL IDEALS IN THE ANCIENT WORLD (Grand Rapids, MI: Baker Book House, 1959) pp.43.45.

41. William J. Bennett WHAT WORKS: RESEARCH ABOUT TEACHING AND LEARNING (Washington, D.C.: United States Department of Education, 1986) p.7,19.

PART IV
Biblical Schools for Covenant Children
The Call

There lived at Coventry a little band of serious Christians, four shoemakers, a glover, a hosier, and a widow named Smith, who gave their children a pious education. The Franciscans were annoyed that laymen, and even a woman should dare meddle with religious instruction. On Ash Wednesday (1519) Simon Mourton, the bishop's summoner, apprehended them all, men, women, and children. On the following Friday, the parents were taken to the abbey of Mackstock, about six miles from Coventry, and the children to the Gray Friars convent. 'Let us see what heresies you have been taught,' said Friar Stafford to the intimidated little ones. The poor children confessed that they had been taught in English the Lord's prayer, the apostles' creed and the ten commandments. On hearing this, Stafford told them angrily: 'I forbid you (unless you wish to be burnt as your parents will be) to have anything to do with the Pater, the credo or the ten commandments in English.'

Five week after this, the men were condemned to be burnt alive, but the judges had compassion on the widow because of her young family (for she was their only support) and let her go. It was night. Mourton offered to see Dame Smith home; he took her arm, and they threaded the dark narrow streets of Coventry. 'Eh. eh!' said the summoner on a sudden, 'What have we here?' He heard in fact the rattling of a scroll within her sleeve. 'What have you got there?' he continued, putting his hand up her sleeve, from which he drew out a parchment. Approaching a window whence issued the faint rays of a lamp, he examined the mysterious scroll, and found it contained the Lord's prayer, certain articles of faith, and the ten commandments in English. 'Oh, oh! sirrah!' said he; 'come along. As good now as another time!' then seizing the poor widow by the arm, he dragged her before the bishop. Sentence of death was immediately pronounced on her, and on the Fourth of April, Dame Smith, Robert Hatches, Archer Hawkins, Thomas Bord, Wrigsham and Lansdale were burnt

alive at Coventry in the Little Park, for the crime of teaching
their children the Lord's prayer, the apostles' creed and the
ten commandments of God."[1]

There is no doubt that biblical Christian education was one of
the utmost values for the Reformation saints. In fact, it has
remained an utmost value to many contemporary Christians.
Marion Snapper has reminded us that early Dutch Christians in
America started Christian schools before they cleared their
farmland.[2] Moreover, for ancient Jews, "of such importance was
education regarded that it was held that even the building of the
temple could be interrupted before education was interrupted.
'Perish the sanctuary but let the children go to school.' ... [and]
it has always to be remembered that Jewish education was
entirely religious education."[3]

We believe that the above historical examples of commitment
to biblical education are founded upon and deeply rooted in the
covenant relationship which God has established with His
people by His Spirit. In other words, biblical Christian education
is our covenantal responsibility. There is no alternative lest we
ignore, suppress, reject or compromise the Word of God, the
teaching of the Holy Spirit or our faith commitment to the Lord
Jesus Christ. Consequently, we affirm that all education is
religious education. It is either in concert with God's covenant,
and thus, under His authority, or it stands in direct opposition to
God's covenant. In short, God's covenant, through Christ as
expressed in the Bible, is to be the bride of our children, and
with the imparting of faith by the Spirit, our children are
consummated as a wife in covenant with Almighty God.
Anything less than a full-orbed, biblical education is violation of
our wedded covenant with the Lord Almighty, Maker of heaven
and earth.

This covenant faith-commitment stands at the outset of our
educational ideology. It stands in complete opposition and in
stark contrast to the faith-commitments prescribed by all other
educational ideologies. Although we share the same world or
cosmos with all people, our covenant faith-commitment gives us
a different view of it, which is completely different in thought
and action. It is imperative that we teach this all-comprehensive
difference to our children. They must be guided in all manners
of life to seek first the Kingdom of God and His righteousness.

Samuel Miller of "Old Princeton" wrote, in 1812, statements which clearly illustrate our point. He said, a

> *cruelty* consists in this, that parents, professedly Christian, after having been instrumental in bringing into the world children in their likeness, possessed of a depraved nature, put those children in a place, and under circumstances where the depravity of their nature will rather be cherished and increased, than checked and corrected. . . . Such is *the scope* of true religion; such its *commanding authority;* such its *present,* and its *future, everlasting consequences,* that every department of knowledge is subordinate to it, because it derives its real value from its relation to true religion. Unless it directly or indirectly promotes this religion; unless it aids in illustrating, applying and defending the truths of this religion; unless it cooperates with the specific design of the Bible, to make us seriously and perseveringly engage in glorifying God, and making our light so shine before men, that they may glorify God, it does not deserve our attention; for it is not suited to our *character as men, to our state as dependent and accountable creatures.* . . . What a contradiction to this incontrovertible duty [our covenant responsibility to seek first the kingdom of God and His righteousness] is the conduct of these parents who knowingly and willingly send their children to such instructors as do not believe in the Lord Jesus Christ, and do not live godly in Christ Jesus; to instructors of whom they have no evidence, even in judgment of charity, that they regard the Savior and his cross![4]

Certainly Miller understood the implication's of God's covenant of redemptive grace for the necessity of Christian education. The Lord always carries out His intentions. He exposes the thoughts and actions of men to the light of his purpose, holiness and righteousness. Christians educating their children in accord with the fullness of God's covenant can stand boldly before the Lord because they have not compromised their children to educational infidelity. On the other hand, professing Christians who unite with the sons of perdition are building Tower of Babel public schools. They are entangled with an outward unity of unbelief which stands in the power of the majesty of mankind. How in clear conscience can such parents sing, "*Holy, Holy, Holy! Lord God Almighty! All Thy works shall praise*

Thy Name, in earth and sky and sea; Holy, Holy, Holy!" and suppress its lyrical content in the education of their children. Our educational task is to enhance the words of this song in the teaching-learning ministry of our covenant children.

We seek to stand with the apostle, Paul. He teaches us in the closing words of Romans (Roman 16:24-27) that the Lord Almighty is the power that establishes his students *according to the gospel* and the *proclamation of Jesus Christ,* according to the revelation of the mystery, ... but now *revealed and made known by the scriptures* ... so that all nations might *believe and obey* him - the only wise God be glory forever, through Jesus Christ. Truly, truly it is biblical educators in Christian schools that alone educate in full accord with the gospel, proclaim all the teachings of Christ, reveal and make known the scripture, and believe and obey Him.

We conclude that major overhaul is needed in the educational process used by biblical educators. Biblical pedagogy is a must for our Christian schools. To be sure, over the years various Christian educational philosophers and theologians have proclaimed the covenant foundation for biblical education and have identified its essential components. Nonetheless, it has remained a mystery how to put them into actual practice. Christian educators have failed to set forth a distinctively biblical learning theory. Rather, they have been seemingly content to add, integrate or synthesize biblical principles with educational learning processes which are clearly anti-Christian. Such efforts to Christianize ungodly learning theory must be aborted in favor of building our own biblically distinctive view of learning.

In order to set forth a distinctively biblical view of Christian school education, we advocate that our biblical faith-commitments be clearly set forth at the outset of our total educational system. In other words, everyone has either biblical or nonbiblical faith-commitments which are directive for their thinking and activity. These faith-commitments are completely incompatible and stand in stark contrast. Christian educators must comprehend our biblical faith-commitments which are set forth in Parts I and II of this book. They must build a biblically distinctive view of learning. There can be no cross overs. Biblically directed educators cannot cross over and build truly biblical education while holding to nonbiblical faith-commitments. Unfortunately, Christian educators have extensively crossed over, and thus, built many aspects of Christian schooling on a foundation of non-biblical faith-commitments. Repeatedly I hear, "The public schools do [this or that]." Who cares! The question is, "What does the Bible say about [this or that]." I know of no public school system which carries out its educational system in submission to biblical authority. Perhaps one of the reasons why many Christian parents cross over by sending their children to non-Christian public schools is that Christian school educators have also crossed over and thereby failed to set forth the radical contrast between the two faith-commitments.

As a result of the above stated convictions which are best expressed in our biblical faith-commitments, we propose Ministry-Learning as taught by way of the biblical view of integral pedagogy. We believe that this view is biblical while both the traditional and progressivist views accommodate unbiblical faith-commitments or ignore clear biblical principles. Based upon the eternal covenant, which is fully expressed in the triune Godhead, our view sets forth biblical solutions to educational problems. Clear biblical standards are embraced as absolutes and are always considered relevant. A scriptural view of the learner is constantly set forth as vital to the learning experience. The Holy Spirit is uplifted to His rightful place as Master teacher for Christian students. Student ministry and service tasks are not postponed to the future or reduced to sports entertainment. Actual ministry is a vital part of the daily teaching-learning process. Educating children without these biblical essentials is to submit our children to the dictates of a lesser god than the Creator God of the Bible.

To illustrate my last point, I have before me a *Student Handbook* from a large Christian school. They have over 1,600 students. Their student outreach program is covered with six typed lines while the sports program receives nearly fifty typed lines which includes an open letter from the Superintendent. Perhaps this situation should be reversed. In fact, I believe that biblical Christian schools ought to consider hiring ministry directors before they hire athletic directors and coaches. Could it be that our biblical Christian schools should first build $500,000 ministry centers which are ministry-centered rather than gymnasiums which are entertainment-centered? Clearly all the major athletic objectives could easily be achieved through ministry activities. For example, leadership, teamwork, physical skills, cooperation, stress management and competition are all integral to ministry service. Contrast your local Christian high school's financing and usage of its library with the money and usage for athletics to further illustrate my point. I know of Christian colleges and high schools that have built large gyms before they constructed much needed libraries.

Our view of the change needed for pedagogy to become biblical is broad in scope. It includes the following recommendations.

1. Christian colleges with education departments and teacher-training courses must change their approach to pedagogy. They need to train students in Ministry-Learning teaching views and methods.

2. Christian colleges need to begin practicing Christian integral learning by offering integral units of instruction with special emphasis on ministry projects. Student-teaching must be enhanced by being an actual ministry service. It ought to be a part of every education course.

3. New schools need to be started by parents who desire biblical education for their children. These new schools need to be founded upon God's eternal covenant, express their biblical faith-commitments as up-front and all-comprehensive for all Christian pedagogy, and build upon this biblical curriculum design, methods and learning experiences which are all part of God serving ministry activities.

4. Many Christian schools need to be started in the manner of biblical Ministry-Learning pedagogy. Existing Christian schools need major overhaul and refashioning. Christian school administrators should begin to gradually restructure existing Christian schools according to distinctively biblical designs which are best expressed by Christian Ministry-Learning pedagogy.

5. Christian school teachers may begin to gradually restructure their classrooms and teaching methods to enhance biblical curriculum principles, individualized education, ministry-service projects, the work of the Holy Spirit, skill development,

awareness of faith-commitments, and learning activities which are relevant to actual Christian life.

The above recommendations are stated in brief, general terms. To be sure, they imply major changes in Christian school education, adoption time, a transfiguration of the commonly held concept of Christian pedagogy, and significant advancement in our work for the glory of God. Progress in Christian education will not be easy. Strong, committed, trained and Spirit-directed Christian educators and parents are essential.

Already several college professors have recognized their role and have begun to take the lead by teaching various aspects of Christian integral education. New biblical Christian schools have started in Cincinnati, Charlotte, Pittsburg, Cleveland and Berkley. These schools are at the cutting edge of the advancement of Christian pedagogy. The cutting edge is not adding special education classes, major sports programs, summer missionary teams or high tech music ministries. Furthermore, Christian educators are holding conferences for the purpose of developing authentic and effective biblical Christian schools.[5] Conferences that emphasize the "practical" with pragmatic philosophy and "what works" utilitarian modes of success, that provide "warm, fuzzy feelings" and catchy things to do are insufficient.

A movement is afoot that is advancing beyond the vision found in the old established schools. Believing that Christian schools can do a much better job, many dedicated but discontent Christian educators and parents are moving forward with a new zeal by redesigning Christian school education with biblical changes and improvements.

Francis Schaeffer has stated very clearly:

> The real battle is in the heavenlies. The Scripture, therefore, insists that we cannot win our portion of the engagement with earthly weapons. ... In this war if Christians win the battle by using worldly means, they have lost. On the other hand, when we seem to lose a battle while waiting on God, in reality we have won. The world may mistakenly say, 'They have lost.' But if God's people seem to be beaten in a specific battle not because of sin or lack of commitment or lack of prayer or lack of paying the price but because they

have waited on God and refused to resort to the flesh, they have won.[6]

Therefore, if we apply these biblical principles to pedagogy, we readily see that the real educational battles are in the heavenlies for the minds of children. We can win this battle because Christ has defeated Satan on the cross. In order to win, we must submit to the Holy Spirit's use of biblical principles in our lives and in all our educational practices. We must resist the educational ways of the world and embrace biblical pedagogy for all of God's covenant children. It is treason to transfer the education of covenant children into the hands of pagans. It is also disloyal to the Lord to bring pagan pedagogy into the schools.

> God's sovereignty as King was cosmic, and this cosmic sovereignty demands that all learning in church and school ... acknowledges the sovereignty of the triune God. It is because Christ is King and demands our all, that education at all levels be self-consciously, confessionally Christian. True knowledge of reality cannot be obtained apart from the revealing and regenerating work of God's spirit. Since education equips students for a life of service in the kingdom of God, any education which fails explicitly to acknowledge Jesus as Lord is inadequate. The Kingship of Christ demands Christian education.[7]

NOTES

1. J. H. Merle d'Aubigne THE REFORMATION IN ENGLAND, Vol.I pp.161-162.

2. *Lynden Christian School Keeps Covenant 75 Years* THE BANNER, September 9, 1985, p.24.

3. William Barclay EDUCATIONAL IDEALS IN THE ANCIENT WORLD (Grand Rapids, MI: Baker Book House, 1974) pp.11-13.

4. Samuel Miller BAPTISM AND CHRISTIAN EDUCATION (Jackson, MS: Presbyterian Heritage Publications, 1984) pp.129-130.

5. Nicholas Wolterstorff *Authentically and Effectively Christian,* THE BANNER, September 1, 1986, pp.6-7; and Norman DeJong, ed., CHRISTIAN APPROACHES TO LEARNING THEORY (Lantam, MD: University Press of America, 1984). Note: three annual conferences have been held on Christian learning theory at Trinity Christian College. Others are being planned (Signal Conference for Integral Christian Schools, Pittsburgh, PA, June 22-23, 1987), and the major papers have been published.

6. Francis Schaeffer NO LITTLE PEOPLE (Downers Grove, IL: IV Press, 1974) pp.70-72.

7. John Bolt CHRISTIAN AND REFORMED TODAY (Jordan Station, Ontario: Paideia Press, 1984) p.103.